THE
JUDAS
GOAT

THE
JUDAS
GOAT

PERRY STONE

CHARISMA
HOUSE

Most CHARISMA HOUSE BOOK GROUP products are available at special quantity discounts for bulk purchase for sales promotions, premiums, fund-raising, and educational needs. For details, write Charisma House Book Group, 600 Rinehart Road, Lake Mary, Florida 32746, or telephone (407) 333-0600.

THE JUDAS GOAT by Perry Stone
Published by Charisma House
Charisma Media/Charisma House Book Group
600 Rinehart Road
Lake Mary, Florida 32746
www.charismahouse.com

Unless otherwise noted, all Scripture quotations are from the New King James Version of the Bible. Copyright © 1979, 1980, 1982 by Thomas Nelson, Inc., publishers. Used by permission.

Scripture quotations marked AMP are from the Amplified Bible. Old Testament copyright © 1965, 1987 by the Zondervan Corporation. The Amplified New Testament copyright © 1954, 1958, 1987 by the Lockman Foundation. Used by permission.

Scripture quotations marked KJV are from the King James Version of the Bible.

Scripture quotations marked NIV are from the Holy Bible, New International Version. Copyright © 1973, 1978, 1984, International Bible Society. Used by permission.

Cover design by Justin Evans
Design Director: Bill Johnson

Visit the author's website at www.voe.org.

Library of Congress Cataloging-in-Publication Data:
An application to register this book for cataloging has been submitted
to the Library of Congress.
International Standard Book Number: 978-1-62136-521-1
E-book ISBN: 978-1-62136-522-8

First edition

13 14 15 16 17 — 9 8 7 6 5 4 3 2 1
Printed in the United States of America

I wish to dedicate this book to the greatest woman I have ever known, my lovely companion, Pam. Many people who do not know her background are unaware of the difficult circumstances she encountered as a young teenager, including the divorce of her parents and how a church family took her and her two sisters into their home to live, treating them as their own daughters. Her biological father neither attended her wedding nor walked her down the aisle, yet she has never allowed her past circumstances to determine her future. Since the age of seventeen she has matured into a strong woman of faith and is truly my Proverbs 31 woman—I love her dearly. By her example she has taught others to move on past hurts, betrayals, and disappointments and to live in righteousness and peace—a peace that no man or woman can take from you. She is deserving of great honor as a great woman of God for this generation.

Love you always, Pam,

Perry

Contents

Introduction

I NEVER WILL FORGET a very sad phone call in February of 1990. Our son was about two months old, and my wife, Pam, and I were staying in the pastor's home while conducting an annual revival in Deland, Florida. The voice on the other end of the phone informed us of a tragedy in Alabama. We learned that Pam's closest friend, a precious Italian girl in her early twenties named Tracy, had been instantly killed in a car wreck. To say we were stunned and in total shock is an understatement. We immediately called the family for details, left the revival, and made plans to attend the home-going ceremony near Sumiton, Alabama. Losing your best friend at such an early age was not ever supposed to occur. Tracy had already told Pam she was moving to Cleveland to be close to her and to be in Jonathan's life as his "nanny." While Pam had numerous female friends from Alabama, weeks after the funeral I could see the friendship void created by Tracy's death. My wife is much more relationship driven than me, and I began praying for the Lord to send someone to become as close a friend as Tracy had been to Pam.

As time passed, another young woman moved to town who was well received as a friend by Pam and by my little son, Jonathan. For several months things were going well, and I began to be grateful that finally Pam had a female friend she could hang with, share her burdens with, and just chill out with at times. However, as months passed, the experience with this person proved every person must be cautious as to whom you allow into the inner circle of your friendships. As humans, we often fill our friendship voids by inviting a *first-chair person* to sit in our *third chair*. (See chapter 4, "Who Is Sitting in Your Third Chair?", for detailed understanding.)

The friendship abruptly ended in what I term as a betrayal. Personally I can handle an individual turning against me and I can move on, as I have dealt with negative attitudes and opinions since I was eighteen years of age, but in this case I was very upset that my sweet wife was emotionally hurt by words and actions. (I won't go into detail beyond this point.) For months following, I saw Pam put up a trust barrier. She remained a loving wife and mother, but with the exception of a few staff persons, she did not seek out new friendships. Time passed, and today she has long been removed from any hurt, has erased all possible offense, and has moved forward to become a spiritual mother to a generation of youth. Today she has more true friends than she can keep up with. She has learned, "Forgive and go on."

I identify the act of a person betraying another with what I call *the Judas goat*. When I say the phrase, "He (or she) is a Judas goat," is there a person or persons you know who immediately enter your mind? Christians know from the New Testament that Judas was an inner-circle-apostle-turned-traitor who betrayed Christ to the Jewish religious leaders. So, who in the church has hurt you recently?

As a fourth-generation minister, I believe we could label various members in most churches as *the odd flock*. The church is called the "flock of God" (1 Pet. 5:2–3), with sheep being a metaphor for the members and a shepherd the metaphor for pastors (John 10:11–14). We are an *odd flock*, consisting of sheep, goats, a few barking dogs, and occasional stray pigs. Using the animal metaphor, sheep are believers who faithfully follow the shepherd and enjoy grouping in flocks with other sheep, grazing the green pastures, and drinking from the "living water" of the Holy Spirit (John 4:10). The goats are also a part of any flock grazers and are often seen in Israel intermingling in the same green grass with the sheep. However, because goats and sheep have different personalities, goats often graze among their own groups, as goats tend to be *moody*. On the more negative side, a *dog* is considered a backslider whose actions of turning away from Christ are as a metaphor of a dog returning to his own vomit (2 Pet. 2:22). In the New Testament a swine is a person who is more of a spiritual apostate. We read where Christ instructed:

> Do not give what is holy to the dogs; nor cast your pearls before swine, lest they trample them under their feet, and turn and tear you in pieces.
>
> —Matthew 7:6

The idea of *spiritual goats* in a church has always been intriguing to me, having come from a fourth-generation ministry heritage and being a pastor's son. When Dad would encounter a very disgruntled and overly opinionated church member, we kids would often call them "an old goat," not out of disrespect or due to a person's age, but a term to identify a person who was always *butting heads* with everyone and *nosing into situations* where they were not invited. They gave opinions to questions they were never asked and sought attention to soothe their feelings of neglect. At times the feeling of being neglected was assumed on purpose, for no one in the flock enjoyed the company of an overly opinionated negative mouth.

Then, in every congregation, there was always *the Judas goat*.

Few believers need to read the résumé of Judas Iscariot, the personally chosen apostle of Christ who willfully chose to betray the Savior. It was Judas who served as the treasurer for the ministry team, and when choosing between a woman worshipping Christ or selling her alabaster box for money, he would have chosen the money for the box (Matt. 26:7–13). In fact, John calls Judas a "thief" (John 12:6), the Greek word *thief* being *kleptes*, a general word used in the New Testament for one who steals from others (John 10:1; 1 Thess. 5:2, 4). This overt interest in money and how it was spent was evident in the motivation for Judas to request thirty pieces of silver to betray Christ, turning Him over into the hands of His religious enemies (Matt. 26:15). Judas entered the flock as a sheep, but the agenda in his heart exposed him as a goat.

The Judas goat was the name of an actual goat especially trained to work at a slaughterhouse.[1] The process works as follows: In the case of sheep, the goat is trained to associate and become familiar with the sheep in the field—eating with them, lying down with them, and generally *gaining their trust*. After many months the season arrives for leading the sheep into the slaughterhouse. As the stockyards open, the sheep, in an innocent manner, will follow the Judas goat into specially marked pens or into the back of trucks and, in some instances, into the slaughterhouse itself. The outcome for the goat differs from the sheep—because as the goat leads an entire flock into the slaughter, a special gate is prepared and opened for only the goat, enabling the goat to escape the final gate that leads the others to their deaths. The goat will escape the slaughter, returning to the field where he will begin this *deceptive* process again with a new flock of sheep.

Betrayal by enemies is *expected*, but betrayal by family and friends is *exhausting*. Betrayal will plant seeds of bitterness, which, if left alone, will mature into the fruit of rebellion and resistance. If these seeds are not rooted up and routed out of your mind and spirit, you will move into the desert of unforgiveness, leading you into a barren, fruitless life.

A few times in my life I have been betrayed by people who identified themselves as "best friends" or an "inner circle partner" in our ministry. Having personally experienced hurt, betrayal, hypocrisy, and general disappointment from so-called friends, I have learned much over my lifetime of ministry concerning how to handle and deal with seasons of betrayal, disappointment, discouragement, and unforgiveness caused by Christians. I am convinced that the sin of unforgiveness hinders more believers from their potential and spiritual blessings than any other single weapon of the enemy.

The insights in this book will address the very practical issues mentioned above and will reveal the plan of God in Scripture to bring you healing, wholeness, and freedom from the actions of any Judas goat you have experienced or will later experience.

GOD BLESS YOU,
PERRY STONE

Chapter 1

SLEEPING WITH A GOAT IN YOUR BED

THERE ARE MEN and women, believers who truly love God, who are going to bed each night with a goat. To understand this statement and the danger of sleeping with a goat, we need to understand the use and purpose of goats in the Old Testament.

In the Torah (five books of Moses) the first mention of a goat was when God cut covenant with Abraham and the patriarch of the faith offered "a three-year-old heifer, a three-year-old female goat, a three-year-old ram, a turtledove, and a young pigeon" (Gen. 15:9). In ancient times the female goats were of more value than the males, as the females provided milk and could reproduce small goats, called *kids*. In this light it is somewhat humorous that parents often call their children their *kids*!

Perhaps the most significant indicator of the symbolic meaning of the goat is found in the narrative of Jacob's life. When Isaac was lying on his death bed, his eyes were dim, and his son Jacob covered his hands with the hair of a young goat, tricking his father into believing he was his brother, Esau, who was a very hairy man (Gen. 27:15–29). Thus Isaac was *deceived with goat's hair.* Many years later Jacob was deceived when his eleven sons returned from the field carrying Joseph's torn coat, which had been dipped in the blood of a young goat (Gen. 37:30–33). The same man who deceived his aged father using the hair from a goat was later tricked by his own sons with the coat of his son, also believed to be made of goat's hair and dyed with different colors.

Thus Jacob, who would later be called *Israel* (Gen. 32:28), was deceived by goat's blood, and his father was deceived by goat's hair. These two narratives are believed to be linked to the reason the high priest selected the two goats for the atonement offering on Yom Kippur, the Day of Atonement.

> He shall take the two goats and present them before the LORD at the door of the tabernacle of meeting. Then Aaron shall cast lots for the two goats: one lot for the LORD and the other lot for the scapegoat. And Aaron shall bring the goat on which the LORD's lot fell, and offer it as a sin offering. But the goat on which the lot fell to be the scapegoat shall be presented alive before the LORD, to make atonement upon it, and to let it go as the scapegoat into the wilderness.
> —LEVITICUS 16:7–10

On the Day of Atonement two identical goats were selected to stand before the high priest. One goat was marked "for the Lord" and was slain on the brass altar, and the other was a scapegoat. The high priest placed his hands upon this goat's head, transferring the sins of Israel upon the goat. Afterward this goat was led into the wilderness by other priests and eventually pushed off a cliff on a hill twelve miles from Jerusalem called the "Mount of the Azazel," as the name is said to mean "strong and mighty," referring to the large mountain from which the goat was pushed and met its death. The name Azazel was also considered to be the name of the demon that carries with it the sins of Israel back to Satan, a thought that is found in the ancient Jewish Book of Enoch 8:1.[1] The reason for using two goats is that the first goat atoned for the people's sin on the altar, and the scapegoat was sent out to remove the sins of the people from their presence. The blood of the first goat brought forgiveness, and the second brought cleansing and righteousness.[2]

The Jewish Talmud indicates that the two goats should be identical in size and appearance.[3] The reason given is that the goats should look similar to twins, as they also represent the twin brothers Jacob and Esau. It is also pointed out that Isaac, the father of Jacob and Esau, requested that Esau go hunting and then cook his father his favorite meal. It was Rebekah who sent the younger Jacob to bring the "two choice kids of the goats," requested by Isaac so that he "may eat, that my soul may bless you before I die" (Gen. 27:1–10).

There is also an interesting link to the Hebrew words used in the Genesis narrative. In Genesis 27:11 Esau is called, a "hairy man." The Hebrew word for "hairy" is *sair*. The word for "goat" in Hebrew is *sa'iyr* and refers to a male goat. Thus Esau was hairy like a goat, revealing why Jacob used goat's hair, and Isaac was deceived when feeling the goat hair covering Jacob's hand. This is why the goat in the earliest times was considered an animal of deception.

Under the old covenant, when the scapegoat was pushed from the top of the cliff and rolled to its death from the Mount of Azazel, the sins of the people were forgiven and removed. A tradition developed in Israel whereby the high priest would place a long crimson wool thread (about eighteen inches long) on the neck of the goat being offered on the altar, and one red thread tied between the horns of the scapegoat.[4] In the early days it was believed the scapegoat was simply turned loose after the priest transferred the sins upon the goat's head. But if the goat lived, it could wander into a village or city in Israel, carrying with it the past sins of Israel. Thus the goat met its death in the wilderness. God was insistent that the goat bearing the sin would not be free to roam from village to village, bringing the iniquities back upon the people who were released from them.

LIVING WITH A GOAT IN YOUR HOUSE

What does the history of these goats have to do with a *goat in your own house*? In the New Testament Christ was teaching His disciples the importance of forgiving persons who offend them. When asked how often a person should forgive a brother who offends that person, Christ answered, "Seventy times seven" (Matt. 18:22), which implies that as often as a person asks for forgiveness, we must be willing to forgive.

After Christ's resurrection He gave a very interesting statement to His disciples:

> And when He had said this, He breathed on them, and said to them, "Receive the Holy Spirit. If you forgive the sins of any, they are forgiven them; if you retain the sins of any, they are retained."
>
> —JOHN 20:22–23

The Amplified reads:

> [Now having received the Holy Spirit, and being led and directed by Him] if you forgive the sins of anyone, they are forgiven; if you retain the sins of anyone, they are retained.
>
> —JOHN 20:23, AMP

This verse is not intended to indicate that a believer can walk around telling other people their sins are forgiven, as Christ did in His earthly walk, since only Christ is our heavenly priest and provided atonement for mankind's sins, and He alone has the power to forgive and cleanse a sinner. This speaks to us of an individual who sins against us personally or causes an offense with us. When a believer asks for your forgiveness for a trespass or an offense, when you forgive them, then forgiveness immediately occurs. However, if we refuse to forgive, then those sins are retained by us and not forgiven. What we refuse to forgive causes us to enter the realm of unforgiveness, which, in the New Testament, is a sin and carries spiritual consequences.

The word *remit* in the Greek is *aphiemi* and means, "to send forth and to go forth." In the New Testament the word *remission* is used in ten passages, and in nine of the ten the word is used referring to pardoning sins (Matt. 26:28; Mark 1:4; Luke 1:77; 3:3; 24:47; Acts 2:38; 10:43; Heb. 9:22; 10:18). If you were living in the time of the tabernacle of Moses or of the first and second temples in Jerusalem, the imagery of remitting a person's sins would have been clearly demonstrated by the imagery of the Day of Atonement (Yom Kippur), when the sins of the entire nation were transmitted to the scapegoat as the high priest prayed a prayer of remission, laying his hands upon the goat's head. To forgive is equated with sending forth the goat bearing sin away from you!

When a believer walks in unforgiveness by refusing to remit the offenses of others, that person is symbolically taking the scapegoat bearing the transgression into his or her home and living with the old goat! As illustrated earlier, Israel eventually established a tradition of pushing the scapegoat off the cliff, as sins that were remitted to the goat must never be brought up again and must forever be removed from the land of Israel. God declared: "I, even I, am He who blots out your transgressions for My own sake; and I will not remember your sins" (Isa. 43:25). If God chooses to forgive and forget, then we must choose to do likewise.

Take, for example, two church members who engage in a major disagreement, leading to an argument that severs their friendship. Opposing opinions have cut the cord of unity, and both have ceased speaking to one another, avoiding any form of fellowship. Each is now campaigning in secret to pull other friends into their offense and to agree with their side of the argument. This strife leads to unforgiveness, which brings a *goat* into their lives. Each evening when they return from work, they are dragging the goat with sin into their front door. As they eat dinner, there is the old goat near them, bringing up the smells of the past. When the unforgiving person lies in bed at night, the old ugly goat of unforgiveness is plopping on the covers at the foot of the bed. *The only way to remove the goat is to remove the offense!*

THE JUDAS GOAT IN YOUR LOCAL CHURCH

The apostle Judas was selected in the position of treasurer in Christ's traveling evangelistic ministry. He was a goat in the midst of the sheep. At times the Judas goat will warm the front pew during services, fold its arms in resistance in the front row of the choir, and perhaps even serve on the board of elders! The Judas goat is a master at butting into situations and using its horns to push its way into and out of the flock, especially when there are important decisions to be made. In the Bible horns represent political and spiritual authority of a king, a kingdom (Rev. 13:1–2), or of a religious leader such as the future false prophet—the lamb with two horns (v. 11). Both sheep and goats have horns, although rams have curved horns and only certain breeds of sheep have horns. Because of the disposition of goats, it has been suggested that people who own goats should remove the horns. Although they are beautiful animals, goats learn to use their horns as an offensive tool, goading other animals and even humans. At times a horned goat can be in a playful mode and yet unknowingly harm a person by injuring him with its horns.[5]

The parallel spiritual principle of the goat's horns is that in local congregations there are often individuals who desire to exercise their "authority" by causing some form of discord among others, leading to spiritual wounds and emotional pain through cutting words. A Judas goat is not concerned if a church loses members or attendees as long as his or her territorial control is not threatened.

Throughout my father's ministry he pastored some of the greatest Christians I have ever met, individuals whose lives reflected Christ and the Scriptures. However, in every congregation there were one to three of the Judas goats. I can recall on one occasion that Dad was preaching against racism and was approached by two members of the church, both men, who asked to speak with him in private outside the church. When the three stepped outside the front door, one threatened, "Preacher, if you know what is good for you, you will never mention racism again."

Dad boldly reminded those men that he was the pastor and would preach whatever the Spirit of the Lord placed in his heart to minister. The second man reached into his wallet and pulled out a card indicating he was a leader in the KKK in that county.

Unimpressed, Dad responded, "If I were you, I would go home and burn that card!"

The older man replied, "Preacher, if you don't take heed to our orders, you may just find your house burnt down!" These two men were not just Judas goats, but both were bordering on being *spiritual swine*. (See 2 Peter 2:20–22.)

A week later on Sunday morning, one of these two men carried a gun into the church under his coat, which at that time and in that state was illegal to bring into a church. When Dad was informed, he went into his church office and called the police station, telling the dispatcher that a man was in the church carrying a gun without a permit. Dad requested, "Is it possible for you to send me two of the tallest and strongest black police officers to the church?" When questioned why, Dad said, "They will understand when they get here." In a few moments two tall and very strong black police officers were in the lobby. Dad led them to the back pew, pointing out the Judas goat. The man went into a rage, and the officers led him out flaying like a mad man. Dad headed to the pulpit and carried on with the service. Needless to say, Dad didn't stay at that church long, leaving shortly thereafter. He discovered that particular congregation seemed to be a breeding ground for goats instead of a field of sheep.

LEAD THE GOAT AWAY FROM YOUR LIFE

After the high priest transferred Israel's sins upon the head of the scapegoat, a rope was tied to the neck of the goat, and a priest would run with the goat across a three-tiered bridge linking the Eastern Gate with the Mount of Olives, heading into the Judean wilderness far away from the sacred temple in Jerusalem. (See

Leviticus 16.) Along the way a series of way stations were set up with ten booths at equal distances to ensure that the mission was accomplished and where food and drink were offered, but each time the priest leading the goat would refuse. The entire day was set aside for a national fast.[6] Without the goat being led away from God's presence into the dry, barren desert, symbolically the sins of Israel would remain as long as the goat was living.

Forgiving others is a *command* but also a *choice.* I do not forgive because I feel a sudden unction or excitement to do so, but because I choose to do so. Repenting of your own sin is a *command*, as it is written, "But now [God] commands all men everywhere to repent" (Acts 17:30). It is also a *choice,* as it is written, "Choose for yourselves this day whom you will serve" (Josh. 24:15).

There are several reasons why people refuse to release others who have trespassed.

1. We believe we are in the right and they are in the wrong, and we wait for the other person to *get the revelation* of the error of their ways, humbling himself or herself before us and confessing he or she was in the wrong. If you wait for the other person, you may go to your grave disappointed.

2. The second reason we hold back is the idea that the other person is so wrong in his attitude that God will judge him for his actions, and thus we leave him alone in hope that God will *smite him* in some manner to teach him a lesson and bring him crawling back to say, "I am sorry."

3. The third reason is we do not understand the importance of forgiveness, that it is not just *to release* the

other person, but forgiving others is actually for us, to prevent our blessing from being restrained and hindered through unforgiveness.

4. The fourth reason is a five-lettered word called p-r-i-d-e! Our love for self and our personal ego are stronger than our common sense and spiritual motivation. If I am commanded in the Word, then I must choose to agree with and follow the command to release the blessing of the covenant.

How to Forgive in a Terrible Situation

There are situations in which it becomes difficult to release the person who committed the trespass. A man who murders a child, a child molester, a man who rapes a woman, and a relative who sexually abused a near relative are types of transgressions that create holes in the soul and unseen emotional scars. Emotions are the strongest form of ties that bind or of knives that cut and separate that we as humans carry. These wounds are so strong that we read:

> A brother offended is harder to win than a strong city,
> And contentions are like the bars of a castle.
> —PROVERBS 18:19

One reason forgiving the offender in these situations is challenging is the false impression of the offended that forgiving the offender releases the guilty party from judgment for the terrible actions committed, and we the offended would much rather see jail time or punishment enacted for a criminal type of trespass. We desire God to judge the Christian responsible for the hurt.

Forgiveness is not intended to bring *justification* to the offense, as "woe to that man by whom the offense comes" (Matt. 18:7)! Unforgiveness restrains spiritual blessing, thus forgiveness is for your benefit to release spiritual blockades hindering your blessings from flowing.

HE WAS TROUBLED FOR FORTY YEARS

We often fail to realize that a contentious division and wrong actions can also impact the *offender* as much as the offended. Once offended or emotionally damaged, we often feel that the one causing the harm went on with his or her life without any emotional or spiritual repercussions.

My father once shared an incident from the late 1940s in which two young men—one a new convert to Christ and the other a drunken sinner—engaged in a personal conflict one night at a local church, causing a major offense that drove the new Christian to separate himself from the Christian faith and the church for forty years. After forty years had passed, these two men *accidentally* came across one another in a small mountain café. The one man who had initiated the conflict years prior, now over sixty, recognized the other fellow, walked over, and began to speak to him. He said, "Do you remember the incident forty years ago at the church when I was a heathen and came in threatening people? I heard that you left church and never returned. Afterward I was embarrassed and moved from the town myself." The offender had eventually received Christ, and he now confessed to the man he had offended what had bothered him for many years. He said, "All these years I have wondered if you were alive and if you had died without the Lord! At times I was tormented for my stupid actions as a rebellious youth, and I have lived with condemnation all of these years, not knowing if you ever returned to the Lord, or if I would answer to God on the Day of Judgment for your soul."

Dad said, "The backslidden Christian carried an *offense* for forty years, but the offender carried *condemnation* for the same forty years!" The one offended was unaware of the offender's personal, spiritual pain and guilt he bore for his words and actions. Life may have gone on, but the offender's life was not the same until that day he asked for forgiveness from the person he had assaulted four decades prior.

When an offender's actions has affected the life, home, or marriage of a person, we often think that person simply continues on his or her journey, erasing any memory of the actions, thus avoiding any emotional, spiritual, or mental anguish. For a moment imagine an older man who molested a young girl in the family, and years later he sees the same person, now a grown woman with children, and knows she is aware of what he did. Or a mother who abused her children and is now aged and watching the grandchildren, regretting how she treated her kids, yet knowing she cannot undo the past. Our actions when we were younger will eventually lead us in our older age to times of rejoicing, reflection, or, at times, regret. We can never go wrong when forgiving our enemies or our offenders.

One of the most powerful examples of forgiveness was with Pope John Paul II, who was shot four times at Vatican Square on May 13, 1981, by a Turkish terrorist, losing six pints of blood and almost departing from this life.[7] In an unexpected act the pope later forgave his attempted assassin, Mehmet Ali Agca, and in June of 2000, at the request of the pope, Agca was pardoned by Italian President Carlo Azeglio Ciampi and was afterward extradited to Turkey, where he was imprisoned for another crime committed in the 1970s.[8] Perhaps John Paul felt the same way that Christ felt as He hung dying at the hands of Roman soldiers, or as Stephen felt as he was dying at the hands of Jewish radicals.

It is impossible to *preach* forgiveness without *practicing* forgiveness. Get the goat out of your house, your bed, and your life by releasing the power of forgiveness to those who have offended you!

Chapter 2

THE BETRAYING STRATEGY OF A JUDAS GOAT

C HRIST USED THE imagery of a shepherd who separates his sheep from his goats in the narrative of Christ separating the nations from the good and bad. The sheep were placed on the right and the goats on the left, with the goats being removed from the kingdom (Matt. 25:32–46). In the parable, the good nations are the sheep nations. From a biblical perspective, from the time of the Exodus the lamb was a picture of the Messiah. (See Exodus 12.) The prophet Isaiah used a metaphor of a lamb going to the slaughter to illustrate the Messiah's suffering. He wrote:

> He was oppressed and He was afflicted,
> Yet He opened not His mouth;
> He was led as a lamb to the slaughter,
> And as a sheep before its shearers is silent,
> So He opened not His mouth.
> —ISAIAH 53:7

When a sheep is being led into the slaughterhouse, it is completely unaware of what is about to occur. When a sheep is being sheared for its wool or about to be slain for its body, the animal is silent. When Christ the Messiah was being questioned by Herod, He refused to answer his questions—thus fulfilling Isaiah's prophecy of opening not His mouth (Luke 23:7–9).

The Judas goat is a metaphor for a person who gets in the inner circle of a family, church, or ministry looking right, acting right, worshipping right, and giving of his or her time and financial offerings—a perfect example of someone *who looks and acts a little different* but otherwise is viewed as a really good member of the *flock*. Eventually these individuals gain the trust of the leadership and work their way up the ladder of visual recognition and trust. They may be an active part of the congregation for many years. However, when the time comes to choose between being loyal to the ministry or minister, and choosing a better thing for themselves, they always choose the path that looks better for them, being totally unconcerned for the baby lambs and sheep they may hurt in their decision process. They walk through a self-made gate of escape on to greener pastures, leaving the sheep dumfounded, thinking: "How did this happen?" "How could they do this to us?"

The Judas goats in the church have done more to run people away from the church than any other single group or situation. It is one thing for believers to identify a hypocrite. A hypocrite is called a hypocrite because people see the double standard and two-faced lifestyle in a person. The Greek word for "hypocrite" is *hupokrites,* and it refers to a stage actor who performed in the theater, speaking through a large mask with a mechanical device that enhances the volume of the voice for the audience.[1] Christ used the word fifteen times in Matthew, especially exposing the Pharisees as hypocrites for not practicing their own teaching, which they demanded others to follow. However, a Judas goat is often difficult to detect until the day that trouble strikes the church and the sheep are being sheared while being abused for selfish purposes.

Growing up, we had our own Judas goats in churches where my dad pastored. My father, Fred Stone, began his ministry as an evangelist, moving into the position of a pastor after we children came along. I clearly recall Dad pastoring in the rural community of Big Stone Gap, Virginia; Alexandria, Virginia; and Salem, Virginia, a town in the Roanoke Valley, for a total of about nineteen years of pastoral ministry during my childhood and teen years. In each local church were precious, very godly, praying members whom any shepherd would be proud to call his sheep. However, especially in northern Virginia, there were a few men whose attitudes and aggressive opinions were more goat-like than sheep-like. There were several occasions during those years of ministry that church members betrayed their verbal promises and commitments, causing great hurt as they departed from the church. They supported the church as long as they got their way and were in authority, but when their horns were trimmed, they butted heads with the sheep, leaving them dazed as they found other pastures to graze in.

WHY DO PEOPLE BETRAY OTHERS?

In the 1611 King James Version of the New Testament the word *betray* is mentioned seventeen times. In sixteen of the seventeen times the verse refers to Judas Iscariot, the disciple who betrayed Christ. The Greek word for "betray" is the same in all seventeen passages, the word *paradidomi*, which means, "to surrender, yield up or transmit."

To betray a trust is to *surrender information* about a situation or a person to another person. To betray a friendship is to *give up a friend* and separate from someone who has built a relationship in your life. To betray a marriage is to break a vow that was made between the husband and wife. Betrayal is very difficult to overcome, as it breaks the trust that bonds relationships.

We often hear the word *trust* used when someone says, "Trust me when I say…," "You can trust me…," "Trust that product…," and so forth. There are several Hebrew words translated as *trust* in the English Bible.

1. In Psalm 7:1 the psalmist spoke, "O LORD my God, in thee do I put my trust: save me…" (KJV). This word *trust* is *yasha'*, which comes from a root word meaning, "to be open, wide, or free." Consider this meaning, then reflect on the fact that a person must *open his or her heart and spirit up* to another person when trusting them.

2. The psalmist wrote in Psalm 11:1: "In the LORD put I my trust: How say ye to my soul, Flee as a bird to your mountain?" (KJV). This word *trust* in Hebrew is *chacah*, from a root meaning, "to flee for protection in the sense of confiding in." This type of trust is when we trust God to be our refuge in the time of trouble. When we have placed confidence in friends, we trust them enough to also protect our integrity and reputation and we confide in them, both public and private information.

When a person is betrayed, then the betrayer has *surrendered information* that was given in trust, opening and exposing his or her friend's heart during the friendship. If a known enemy works against us, we have little concern for the enemy's opinions, as the old expression says, "There was no love lost," because there was never a relationship or friendship from the beginning. Throughout his lifetime David experienced the knife of betrayal after several of his closest friends turned against him. He wrote:

> For it is not an enemy who reproaches me;
> Then I could bear it.
> Nor is it one who hates me who has exalted himself
>   against me;
> Then I could hide from him.
> But it was you, a man my equal,
> My companion and my acquaintance.
> We took sweet counsel together,
> And walked to the house of God in the throng.
> —PSALM 55:12–14

The enigma of Christianity is that for a religion based upon the mixture of mutual love, honor, and respect, why is there often a lack of all three among Christian brethren? The answer is found in a prediction Christ gave, warning His disciples of events prior to His return:

> And then many will be offended, will betray one another,
> and will hate one another.
> —MATTHEW 24:10

The root cause of betrayal is offense. The Greek word for "offend" is *skandalizo* and means, "to set a trap to ensnare something." We derive the word *scandal* from this word. A scandal occurs when a person or persons betray the trust and confidence of others through words or actions. Some of America's most noted national scandals are the Watergate break-in under the

Nixon Administration, the moral failure of President Bill Clinton, and the incident that was classified by many as a cover-up that occurred when Americans were killed in Libya in late 2012. The longer the press reported the scandals, the more offense they created, especially among those who did not like Presidents Nixon, Clinton, and Obama.

When you become offended, unless you check your attitude, forgive, and move forward, you will begin a betrayal process. Suddenly that best friend becomes a worst enemy, your cherished memories are willfully erased from the hard drive of your memory bank, and the secrets entrusted to each other are now openly discussed with others, using this previously unknown information as a weapon to defend *why* you have a good excuse to remain in your offense.

This is especially true in the ministry, especially when the minister or ministry is globally known. Years ago when three television ministers were engaged in a public conflict, the secular journalists gathered around like a pack of bloodthirsty lions, seeking whom they could devour with their media "inside information." This televangelists' clash was nicknamed "Holy Wars," "Pearly Gate," "Preacher Gate," and every form of title imaginable. During one *exposé* program called *Nightline*, hosted by Ted Koppel, a group of ministers were assembled in a large room to discuss the situation. One of the ministers alleged that the media had set out to destroy these ministries, and if they were to silence their reports, the story would go away. I remember Koppel looking at this ministers' gathering and saying, "The media are getting their information from you ministers."[2] Thus, the red meat being thrown to the hungry wolves of tabloid journalism was being cut up and personally delivered through the written articles and public interviews of ministers themselves.

When offense comes, what is the difference between a person willing to *betray* and *leave* a friend and others choosing to *stay* and *save* the relationship? The answer is simple. It is the genuine love or affection a person has for the individual who has offended or, in some instances, fallen into a moral failure. I observed this once after a noted minister was caught twice in a moral indiscretion, and he reappeared in the pulpit, ministering again. One man who saw him said to me, "I just don't understand why people are still following this man. He messed up twice and yet gets up and goes on like nothing happened."

I replied, "It is because when his ministry was strong, he impacted so many individuals, and those converts are following him now and wish for his restoration. They still love him despite the failures."

True love one toward another restrains offenses from becoming betrayals. Consider your own family. You put up with more *junk* from your children than you would someone else's, and you willingly resist the temptation of throwing your children out when they have rejected your instruction or fallen into sin. You may *discipline* them, but you will not *forsake* them (just as God does not forsake His children) because your love is greater than their foolishness and failures. Discipline is not a sign of rejection but of correction. We read:

> My son, do not despise the chastening of the LORD,
> Nor be discouraged when you are rebuked by Him;
> For whom the LORD loves He chastens,
> And scourges every son whom He receives.
> —HEBREWS 12:5–6

At some point a husband and wife will disagree and argue, and perhaps tempers will flare, but they do not, nor should they, plan for a divorce based upon a series of disagreements. Your boss may agitate you to no end, and you may wish at times you could change jobs, but wisdom tells you to remain calm, complete your assignment, and be thankful your job provides an income. As brothers and sisters in Christ we should treat one another with the same patience and love we have toward our own flesh and blood, as believers are all the family of God. Love will soon erase emotional hurts as it stitches up the wounds and pours in the oil and wine.

Jesus made it clear: "Woe to the world because of offenses! For offenses must come, but woe to that man by whom the offense comes" (Matt. 18:7). From a Greek perspective of the word, an offense, or *skandalon* (the Greek noun), is the bait in the trap that lures the animal into the snare, entrapping it unaware. The purpose of the bait is to allure the animal (or the person) into the trap. In the case of verbal offense where words are used to betray and offend another, it is the reaction of a person to the ensnaring words that either releases him or draws him into the trap.

How your words are received by the *listener* is fascinating and revealing. If a person *loves* the speaker, then the speaker can say nothing wrong, and the listener will defend him even in a questionable statement. If a listener *likes* the speaker, he will give the speaker the benefit of the doubt in a controversial or questionable statement. If a listener does *not at all like* the speaker, then nothing the speaker says or does throughout the service or message is received or accepted, only criticized. This process of acceptance or rejection is based upon *perception*. The act of perception is how you mentally or emotionally *interpret* a person's words or actions.

For example, a leader of a corporation could, in a very

innocent way, pat a person of the opposite sex on the shoulder and say, "Great job, friend." If you have a close relationship and friendship with the patter, you perceive it as a sincere compliment for a job well done and are appreciative of the recognition, as you worked hard to succeed with the project. If you have a casual relationship or friendship, then the gentle pat on the shoulder may be perceived as an unexpected but welcomed sign of appreciation for your work that you seldom receive. If, however, you can't stand the person and wish you did not work there, then you could immediately create the perception of the pat on the shoulder as, "Did you see him touching me? He was coming on to me and harassing me!" The difference between the three perceptions is how the *intent* of the *patter* is properly read or perhaps misread.

A person's *intentions* are the motivation to produce a certain outcome. The intent is the mental reasoning behind the action. For example, it may be necessary for me to confront an issue with one of our staff. My intent is to correct the situation that is causing a possible clash with other workers. When I approach the disgruntled staff, my intent is resolution and not conflict. If the perceiver imagines that I am out to get him or her, then everything I say is filtered in his or her mind as a verbal assault against him or her. The correct perception would be to express appreciation for my concern and to be thankful that my interest is in conflict resolution. The incorrect perception is to feel threatened and believe someone is out to get you.

Even the Bible speaks of two types of manslayers: one who premeditates and plans to slay a man, and one who accidentally kills another fellow human. A premeditated murderer faced a death penalty, but one who slew a man unaware or without wicked intent could flee to a city of refuge and be unharmed until he stood trial and the people heard all the evidence (Num. 35:6–12). This type of action is similar to when a person kills someone in a car accident and can either be charged with voluntary or involuntary manslaughter, depending upon the circumstance, evidence, and intent.

In dealing with staff, volunteers, and people in general for many years, I have discovered that most cases of strife stem from either *misunderstanding* or a *lack of communication*. Also people misread body language. If I hold up two fingers, what does it mean? Stop and think…two fingers? It totally depends upon the context and the setting. In France the two fingers mean peace. In Germany it became a sign of victory after the war. In a major league baseball game the two fingers could mean two hot dogs or two sodas. In a convenience store it could refer to the cost of something being two dollars. When putting them behind someone's head when taking a picture, it's known as "bunny ears" and is poking fun at the person in the picture. However, in some nations such as the United Kingdom, if you hold up two fingers, it is a very offensive gesture. Perhaps you didn't know that holding up two fingers held such a variety of meanings in cultural perception!

My words to you may be spoken with a certain *intent* from my heart. However, your *perception* may not read the true intent, thus giving way to a *misunderstanding*. To "understand" is to correctly comprehend the conversation and correctly interpret its meaning. When the English prefix *mis* is placed in front of the word, it refers to *mistaken, wrong, or incorrect*. Thus a misunderstanding is when you are mistaken in your comprehension of a person's intentions or conversations.

This happens often in a marriage. Women are speakers, and men can be poor listeners. Notice I did not say that men are poor hearers, because we do hear, but there is a process between *hearing* with your ears and listening to the content of the conversation and to what is being said *within* the conversation. Many times my wife has said, "You are hearing me but not listening to what I am saying."

FORGIVING WHEN YOU'VE BEEN "RIPPED OFF"

From my years of traveling, one of the challenges for believers lies in the realm of forgiving an offender who has, as we say, "ripped them off," either through a bad business deal, stolen money, or some Ponzi scheme. The first inclination is to retain a lawyer and head to court. However, at times enormous sums of money can be spent and cases can be lost. What should a believer do when dealing with business that's gone wrong due to the abuse or illegal actions of others?

Strictly from a practical business perspective, a believer should determine if the culprit claims to be another believer or has no claims to the Christian faith and the new covenant. This makes a difference in our approach. As one believer to another, we should be able to settle an issue face-to-face with the understanding that as Christians we are brothers and are required to follow biblical principles of ethics and conduct, reflecting right judgment. If a fellow believer refuses to listen, then a higher level of spiritual leadership, such as the pastor or the pastors from the two individual churches (if one attends another church) should be called together to mediate the issue in an attempt to keep peace. This is based upon a principle and instruction Christ gave:

> Moreover if your brother sins against you, go and tell him his fault between you and him alone. If he hears you, you

have gained your brother. But if he will not hear, take with you one or two more, that "by the mouth of two or three witnesses every word may be established." And if he refuses to hear them, tell it to the church. But if he refuses even to hear the church, let him be to you like a heathen and a tax collector.

—MATTHEW 18:15–17

If both parties are true believers, any financial issue should be settled by godly mediators outside of a legal setting. Paul instructed that two believers should not appear before a court of men (or in a lawsuit), as it becomes a reproach against the name of Christ in the eyes of the unbelievers. When believers fight believers, the unbeliever will comment, "Where is all that Christian forgiveness? I thought Christians are supposed to love each other." Some may say, "They are just like the rest of us." Paul drew attention to this fact:

Dare any of you, having a matter against another, go to law before the unrighteous, and not before the saints? Do you not know that the saints will judge the world? And if the world will be judged by you, are you unworthy to judge the smallest matters? Do you not know that we shall judge angels? How much more, things that pertain to this life? If then you have judgments concerning things pertaining to this life, do you appoint those who are least esteemed by the church to judge?

—1 CORINTHIANS 6:1–4

Biblically, contentious situations are to remain in the church among spiritual leaders who can determine the proper course of action or discipline. True believers will submit to the Word of God and spiritual authority to right the wrongs and correct any conflict. If, on the other hand, the person is an unbeliever, there is another option outside of legal action, which is often not taught or is overlooked—an action that requires real faith and obedience. On one occasion I have taken this action in my own ministry.

When I Was Ripped Off

Years ago I spent many hours working for a businessman to assist him in his business. He was to pay the ministry a certain amount of income for my personal work, as I was not taking the income for myself. When the time came to pay, he made excuses and refused to pay what he owed. After a series of conversations to no avail, I told him I would meet with my board and bring a lawsuit against him, as the money was for much-needed ministry and not me personally. The board was not in favor of a suit, but they said they would follow my desire if I wished.

I remember standing at a mirror shaving when the Holy Spirit impressed me *not* to sue him. The apostle Paul's words in 1 Corinthians 6 kept coming before me. The Holy Spirit impressed me to do something rather odd, which I had never heard of anyone doing. He impressed me to release this man from this debt and to give the money just as though I had given him a financial donation out of the ministry. The Lord impressed me that if I would forgive this man of this debt and release the money to him, the Lord Himself would *double* what was withheld from the ministry. I knew and God knew that this man was wrong, he was operating outside of the Bible, and I would win *in the natural* if I took him to court, but the realm of the Spirit operates under different laws than does the natural realm.

I immediately prayed aloud, "Lord, I forgive this man of this debt he owes, and I sow the money back to him in the name of the Lord!" There were no fireworks or voices from heaven. I simply kept shaving, and that was that. It was not easy to release more than $12,000 that was desperately needed, but I was relieved in my spirit and knew I was obedient to the Word of the Lord. I was just uncertain how the Lord would return double, as our offerings and income were very…and I mean very…limited in that season. At the same time I was reminded of a verse that confirmed what the Spirit had said about receiving a "double return" principle:

> If a man delivers to his neighbor money or articles to keep, and it is stolen out of the man's house, if the thief is found, he shall pay double.
> —Exodus 22:7

In this case I released a man who willfully refused to pay what was owed, and in return I looked to the Lord to give back double. In the natural I knew this was impossible, as our income in those days came from small rural congregations; a few times we had been unable to pay the bills at the end of the month because our income was not enough! Double would be $24,000, which normally could take three months to receive. Months later, however, I can recall going to Leeds, Alabama, where a revival scheduled for one week was moved out of the church under a big tent where it continued for four weeks. The crowds were overflowing into the yard, and people were being converted and baptized in the Holy Spirit nightly. After twenty-eight services, when the offering was given to VOE ministry, several businessmen had given large gifts to help me purchase cassette duplicators, and the check was exactly double of what had been withheld from the ministry. By my forgiving the guilty person, God released a supernatural blessing for doing the right thing.

I have a close friend who is a contractor. In tough economic times it can be challenging for contractors to collect on the work they have completed. In this case the contractor was owed $3,000 and could not collect. The situation was desperate, and the contractor told me, "I don't know that I will ever get that money, and there is not much I can do." I told him, "Write a letter to the man and tell him that if he can live with this on his conscience for the rest of his life, you can live without the money he owes. In this way you will release him to God." He did this and released the situation into God's hands. After he sent the letter, many months passed to no avail, but suddenly the debtor sent him the money and a letter indicating that after he read his letter, he could not sleep at night. He became convicted and wanted to make things right!

In a business in which your life support comes from your work, there will be times of disagreements, broken contracts, bad work, and rip-offs that you, as a believer, must deal with. When being ripped off, it is easy to retaliate and make threats to the debtor or the transgressor. But the best way is to follow spiritual principles and only as a final resort, when absolutely needed, use the legal system to correct detailed legal matters. Under certain circumstances, at times there may be no other option, especially if you are the one being accused or attacked.

There are occasions when a secular (very ungodly) newspaper or journalist attacks a minister's integrity, reporting rumors and unfounded stories of false accounts given to them from "inside sources." Many large gossip tabloids have large sums of money to cover lawsuits and thus at times are able to report the information and worry about the truth after the lawsuit occurs. I recall a ministry friend whose picture appeared in a somewhat compromising manner in a paper. Immediately the body of Christ went wild. What the church did not know is that a person in the ministry who was present was paid huge sums for the picture, and the tabloid had used Photoshop to adjust certain parts of the picture, making it appear as something it was not. To defend their integrity from a very ungodly, lying tabloid, my friend retained several lawyers and won a lawsuit out of court in thirty days, as the tabloid knew they had manipulated the information. When it comes to defending yourself against lies that are distorting your integrity, the only language some in the secular world know is legal language. Remember, unbelievers are not brothers in Christ and are not, in such cases, under the stipulation of Paul's instruction concerning two brothers in Christ.

In the apostle Paul's time the Hebrew believers were being greatly harassed for their conversion to Christ. They were being persecuted, and at times their possessions were taken from them. Paul gave them this word:

> For you had compassion on me in my chains, and joyfully accepted the plundering of your goods, knowing that you have a better and an enduring possession for yourselves in heaven.
>
> —HEBREWS 10:34

Their possessions were on earth, but their treasures were in heaven (Matt. 6:20). I am continually reminded that all we possess on earth remains when we depart to heaven. Believers must continually be reminded that the stuff collected on earth is temporal, and the things we do not see are heavenly and eternal.

The Goats and Sheep
Hear Differently

When a sheep sees a flock of sheep, he sees security. A goat, however, may see an opportunity to take control. When sheep see a shepherd, they see leadership, but when a goat sees a shepherd, he may see a challenge to his own authority. One of the interesting observations between sheep and goats is that when entering a sheep pen, the sheep tend to stay to themselves or with their young and are content to receive food and water. When entering a goat pen, the goats will usually swarm you as though they are competing for your attention. Also, when food is offered to a goat, all of the goats will run toward the food, as though it is each goat for himself. When a shepherd gives the sheep a shot with a needle, they squirm and receive their shot, afterward departing. A goat will continually scream and then will want to be held or gain attention. Goats can be very noisy when they don't like something! Those who raise goats say they can be smart-alecks, mischievous, and always getting into trouble.[3]

The idea of a goat screaming when receiving a shot is humorous for this reason. If you have a pack of dogs and suddenly throw a small stick to break them up, the dog that yelps the loudest is the one that got hit by the stick. When a spiritual goat begins making a lot of noise and negative comments, it may be because something being preached has hit that person and he or she is unable to take the truth.

In the Middle East it is a common scene to watch a shepherd boy herding both sheep and goats. Both are part of a normal flock, and yet sheep and goats have their own distinct habits, routines, and forms of connecting with others in the flock. In the church, where there are sheep, there will also be goats, and if you are seeking to graze in a perfect field (or find a perfect church), you will be continually looking—for when *you* walk through the door with your own spiritual flaws, opinions, and traditions, your field of perfection is suddenly marred by your own humanity. Even sheep—the best and brightest—leave their animal waste throughout the field, and anyone visiting the area must be careful where they step so as to avoid the mess. Wherever there are sheep and goats, there will be places to avoid walking; and wherever you find Christians, there will be some that must be avoided due to the mess they create with their words and deeds.

There are normal goats that mingle with the sheep, and then there is the one Judas goat—the individual or the Judas goat family—within the congregation that thrives on strife, contention, and division; desiring to control the decisions, the music, and the financial giving with manipulation, intimidation, and domination. This includes creating doctrinal rifts and splits among the congregation. Paul dealt harshly with these types in the early church and wrote:

> Now I urge you, brethren, note those who cause divisions
> and offenses, contrary to the doctrine which you learned,
> and avoid them.
>
> —ROMANS 16:17

Division makers are to be *marked* by others within the church. The Greek word for "mark" is *skopeo* and means, "to take an aim at; or figuratively to regard something attentively." From this word we derive our English word *scope*, such as the scope on a gun used to mark a target. Division makers often seek to separate the flock for the sole purpose of gaining their own following. If an individual becomes contentious to the point of dividing the church, they must be warned by the elders, and if they continue in their goat-like aggression, then Paul wrote, "Have no fellowship with the unfruitful works of darkness" (Eph. 5:11).

Great discernment must be applied when dealing with individual believers in a conflict setting. Normal conflicts should be resolved with conflict resolution and wisdom. Believers in a congregation may differ on their eschatology as to when Christ is returning or events surrounding the time of the end. However, this by no means makes a person who disagrees with a prophetic opinion an enemy or *goat*. We need *unity in the flock*. Natural sheep will not drink water unless the water in the brook is still, softly flowing, and clean; also sheep are unable to digest their food if they become uneasy and upset.

An aggressive goat is like a tare in a wheat field. In the parable of the wheat and tares, the wheat is the children of the kingdom, and the tares are the children of the world who are dominated by Satan's thinking (Matt. 13:24–30). Christ said to allow them to grow in the same field, lest by pulling up the tares you destroy the root of the good wheat surrounding the tares (v. 30). Goats are also to remain in the flock, and the Lord Himself will separate them at the time of the end. Sheep are to be loved and cared for and fed with joy, but a goat must be carefully watched and placed on a leash if needed. In a local congregation it is the duty of the shepherd (pastor) and those in spiritual authority to take the goat by the horns, taking control of any situation stirred up or instigated by the negative attitudes and controlling spirits of the church goats.

Chapter 3

WHEN BELIEVERS SIN AGAINST OTHER BELIEVERS

WHAT GOOD WOULD it do to win an argument but to lose the kingdom? Many years ago my father's half-brother, Morgan Ball, was converted to Christ in what was termed the "Coal Field Revival" in the late 1940s. Morgan invited his brother, Fred, to attend. That night Fred answered the altar invitation and began a walk with God that continued until he departed to heaven on March 10, 2011. Shortly after his conversion he and Morgan were at the altar praying when the pastor's son entered the church—drunk, swinging a knife, and making threats. As the pastor's son approached the people, Morgan stood between them and told him to stop talking like he was and simply go outside. The drunken son held up the knife and began cursing Morgan. Suddenly he lunged, and Morgan grabbed him. Instead of rebuking his drunk son, the pastor grabbed Morgan and told him to back up and leave his son alone. An argument ensued, and Morgan was so frustrated that he cursed and walked out of the church; for many years he refused to attend another church service. The drunk son may have won his argument, but Morgan almost lost the kingdom. Forty years later Morgan repented, and before his death he attended my dad's funeral and confessed he was following Christ.

Thousands of church members and attendees may be sinning against other believers, thus endangering their future blessings and positions in the kingdom of God. Many believers have the church routine down pat, but they ignore their own attitudes. This one sin, if not repented, can cause your worship to become noise, your prayers to be hindered, and your preaching to be useless. Here are the important words of Christ to His followers:

> Not everyone who says to Me, "Lord, Lord," shall enter the kingdom of heaven, but he who does the will of My Father in heaven. Many will say to Me in that day, "Lord, Lord, have we not prophesied in Your name, cast out demons in Your name, and done many wonders in Your name?" And then I will declare to them, "I never knew you; depart from Me, you who practice lawlessness!"
>
> —MATTHEW 7:21–23

> And whenever you stand praying, if you have anything against anyone, forgive him, that your Father in heaven may also forgive you your trespasses. But if you do not forgive, neither will your Father in heaven forgive your trespasses.
>
> —MARK 11:25–26

OFFERING SACRIFICES WITH STRIFE

In Proverbs we read:

> Better is a dry morsel with quietness,
> Than a house full of feasting with strife.
>
> —PROVERBS 17:1

This passage is penned by Solomon in the Book of Proverbs—a book classified by scholars as *wisdom literature*. In Proverbs Solomon wrote extensively on the subject of the tongue and how your spoken words hold the power of life and death (Prov. 18:21). The above passage can be applied to a local church in this manner. It is better to sit quietly in a rather dry church service than to experience a church that's celebrating worship by offering the "sacrifice of praise" (Heb. 13:15) but the people's hearts are filled with strife!

This concept was understood in the Old Testament, where various animal sacrifices and offerings were established under the Law and were practiced daily, weekly during the feasts, or during new moons and festivals. God required that the worshipper select the finest sheep from his flock, one without any physical blemish or infirmity (Lev. 1:3, 10; 3:1, 6; 4:3, 23, 28, 32). To be without blemish was to be unspotted, sound in body, and undefiled. However, as the rituals became routine and the routines became a rut, the *process* of worship became more important than the *presence* of the One being worshipped. By the time of the prophet Malachi, neither the priests nor the people understood the divine instruction or the true purpose of the sacrifices, as we read:

> "You offer defiled food on My altar,
> But say,
> 'In what way have we defiled You?'
> By saying,
> 'The table of the LORD is contemptible.'
> And when you offer the blind as a sacrifice,
> Is it not evil?
> And when you offer the lame and sick,
> Is it not evil?

Offer it then to your governor!
Would he be pleased with you?
Would he accept you favorably?"
Says the LORD of hosts.

—MALACHI 1:7–8

The people were willing to give a sacrifice believing God would not notice the corruption and sickness of their offerings. In reality, they were offering the Lord something He not only did not want but also was not receiving. What looked right to men looked wrong to God. What was called *consecration* to men was considered *contemptible* to the Almighty. Today we are not offering the blood from lambs, rams, bulls, and birds, but our sacrifices are the words of worship, giving, and ministering to others. How can we expect the Lord to receive our hymns, fabulous musical compositions that fill the atmosphere, and the sound of thunderous praise when our mouths are filled with shouts yet our hearts are filled with strife?

James summed up the dangers of contention among believers when he wrote, "For where envying and strife is, there is confusion and every evil work" (James 3:16, KJV). The Greek word for "confusion" means, "instability and disorder." On one occasion the disciples engaged in a discussion that led to strife as to who was the greatest in the kingdom (Luke 22:24, KJV). The Greek word for *strife* here is different than in James 3:16. In Luke 22:24 the word is *philoneikia*, meaning, "a dispute and quarrel." In any situation, strife leads to confusion and disputing and "every evil work."

Even in the early church the New Testament records several contentious disputes between leadership. Paul and Peter were in a serious disagreement over the necessity of circumcision for the Gentiles (Gal. 2:9–13). Barnabas separated from Paul over his treatment of a young minister named John Mark (Acts 15:39). Later in life, toward Paul's death, he requested to see John Mark and desired he be brought to Rome, as he was "profitable to me for the ministry" (2 Tim. 4:11, KJV). Apparently this previous contention was so serious that Paul desired to amend his fellowship with John Mark prior to his departure to heaven.

Solomon taught that a contentious person is like one throwing burning coals on a fire (Prov. 26:21). He also wrote that it would be better to dwell in a wilderness (there's that dry place again) than in the same house with a contentious companion (Prov. 21:19). Since God is not the author of confusion (Greek, "disorder and instability"; 1 Cor. 14:33) but of peace, and since strife breeds confusion, then strife is never from the Lord.

Here in Cleveland, Tennessee, we have a ministry called The Extreme and OCI (Omega Center International). It is a combination of youth and adults who meet together for worship, hearing the Word, and fellowship. We have several hundred, including a council of twelve youth leaders whom my wife, Pam, and I love and appreciate. However, as the *father* of the ministry, I have informed them that I have no time for division, strife, or drama. I said: "If you love drama, you are in the wrong place. Join the drama team at Cleveland State or Lee University, but we won't have emotional drama and bickering here!"

The younger generation must become as the children born in the wilderness in the time of Moses. These wilderness babies heard their parents complain, eventually causing God to restrain them from entering their inheritance in the Promised Land. Their children, however, took thirty-one cities with Joshua as their commander, and not once was there a committee of the disgruntled organized to complain! Joshua was more than eighty years old when the nation crossed the Jordan, and he knew he didn't have another forty years to tour the desert. He did not desire a rerun of where he had been but was prepared to believe God and take the land!

When conquering Jericho, the Israelites were defeated at Ai, a small city. Joshua was unaware that one of his men had secretly sinned by collecting forbidden items and hiding them. Joshua became upset and blamed God for the defeat. Basically God revealed the hidden sin and told Joshua to shut up, get up, and take care of the iniquity problem, and then the men in the army would win the war. (See Joshua 7.)

To church members who are directing the drama team by always stroking the embers of rumors and gossip, I suggest that you repent, then shut up, get up, and simply love God, love people, and do the work. Paul addressed the issue of strife in the church at Corinth, reminding them that if they did not love one another, all of their spiritual gifts and work were as a "sounding brass or a clanging cymbal" (1 Cor. 13:1).

THE STORY OF TWO MINISTERS

Years ago there were two ministers with highly successful media ministries. One owned a very large Christian network, and the other had a daily program aired around the world. The evangelist had a paid program on the Christian network, but during his teaching he or others would often make negative and cutting comments against the network they were on! Eventually, after several warnings to the evangelist, the Christian network owner removed the minister from his network, which at that time was reaching about fifteen million homes.

It was some time later that over the network the evangelist confessed to having had an inappropriate relationship, and that information was reported on the secular news. I remember a well-known evangelist being interviewed on a secular network and being questioned about the moral failure of one of his fellow televangelists. I specifically recall this evangelist looking in the camera and, without blinking, calling the fallen minister "a cancer in the body of Christ." At that moment a chill swept over my back, and I turned to my wife and said, "He should never make such a statement. He will fall into the same sin because he has announced his own judgment on a man who has already repented."

A few years later the judgmental minister was caught in a terrible moral sin that was also blasted before the world on major networks and was the feature in many mainstream magazines. Both men publicly repented to the body of Christ and their friends for their sin and asked both God and people for forgiveness, which was the right thing to do. However, I often wondered if the evangelist ever asked the other minister to forgive him for calling him a "cancer in the body of Christ" when he was himself secretly practicing sin.

It would be more than twenty-five years later that I was with the minister who was called the "cancer." He had repented, was restored, and was rebuilding on a solid foundation, ministering to people and mentoring the next generation. Without bringing up the past failure, I did ask one question, and that was, "Did the minister who publicly called you a cancer ever ask you for forgiveness?"

The man smiled and said, "No, and I don't really ever expect him to." He replied, "It is just not in some people's personality to ask for forgiveness."

I replied, "It's simply pride," and immediately we changed the conversation to more edifying spiritual matters.

Using this as an example, one of the sins of the accusing minister was to bring up a man's sin that had already been confessed and repented of. The second aspect is when a person judges another for failure when he is secretly battling the same sins he is criticizing in others. In the early church the apostles and early prophets were committed to teaching others that every teacher must live what they are teaching to others. In the *Didache* (written about AD 120) there is a statement that reads:

> Every prophet who teaches the truth, but does not do what
> he teaches, is a false prophet.[1]

We think of a false prophet as someone who teaches false doctrine or teaches contrary to the Bible. However, when a teacher begins to teach for others to live a certain way, and does not himself live that way, then he is classified as a false teacher or a false prophet. If I were to teach prayer and never pray, expect you to tithe and never give tithes myself, and reveal from the Bible that you should not miss attending God's house and never show up myself, then I am a false teacher. Christ taught that we should never attempt to remove the mote out of our brother's eye when we have a large pole of wood sticking out of our own eye. James 3:10–11 also instructs that out of the same mouth come blessing and cursing, and this should not be.

THE BIBLE ON DISOBEDIENCE

Biblically there are four significant words linked to the concept of disobedience against God and sins. Often we place these words in the same "pot," yet they are all unique with a specific definition. These four words, with their Greek meanings, are shown below:

1. The first word is *sin*, used in the singular form 448 times in the English Bible. The Greek word for "sin" is *hamartia* and generally is understood to mean, "to miss the mark; an archer who aims for the target and shoots the arrow, only to discover he totally missed the mark." It means to go off course and be moved away from the right direction.

2. The word *trespass* is found in the English Bible eighty-two times in the singular form. The Greek word for "trespass" is *paraptoma* and refers to someone passing over and going beyond their rights. We would say crossing a line they were not supposed to cross. People place "No Trespassing" signs in their yards to prevent people from *crossing* into their land.

3. The third word is *transgression*, which is used fifty-one times in the singular form in the Bible. The Greek word for "transgression" is *parabasis*; it is not just choosing to cross the line but to intentionally disobey by crossing the line. It is to willfully choose to do what is forbidden.

4. The fourth word, *iniquity*, is found 278 times in the singular form. The Greek word is *anomia* in Greek and alludes to the willful breaking of the law. It is someone who knows they should not do something and chooses to do it without any fear of the consequences. It is someone who is not falling into sin but is practicing a lifestyle of sin.

All sin has a spiritual root. In Leviticus 4 Moses spoke of a sin of ignorance. The root of this sin is an ignorance of the Scriptures. Often a new convert will have asked Christ into his life yet still act in a manner contrary to what the Scriptures teach. I have known of couples who had no Christian family or biblical foundation who received Christ and continued to live together until they were informed they should either live separately or marry. They honestly did not know their actions were wrong.

In 1 Timothy 6:9 Paul wrote of falling into sin and being overcome by temptation, which is the root force pressuring the person to sin. Paul wrote in Hebrews 10:26 of willfully sinning, which is to volunteer your mind, body, and spirit, giving in to tempting thoughts. Often the root motivation for people who willfully sin is *pride*. David speaks of sins of presumption in Psalm 19:13. Israel was commanded not to go to battle, but the Israelites did so anyway against God's instruction and were defeated. This was presumption on their part, and the root force behind sins of presumption is rebellion.

The greatest majority of preaching on forgiveness and repentance is focused upon having individuals ask God to forgive them of sins, transgressions, and iniquities. However, much was taught in the New Testament of how believers should treat other believers and about sins against believers. From my seventy-five thousand hours of biblical study and research I have concluded that:

1. We must ask God to cleanse us and forgive us of sin to enter the kingdom of heaven.

2. We must ask people to forgive our trespasses in order to receive answered prayer, financial blessing, and increase.

3. We must forgive ourselves to be free spiritually and emotionally from condemnation and guilt.

In the body of Christ the biggest sin is how we mistreat, misspeak, and use negative words against those whom we call our brothers and sisters in Christ. Let me explain why Satan enjoys using Christians to verbally assault other believers.

Satan is called the "accuser of the brethren." Believers who know their covenant relationship with God and are biblically familiar with their archenemy Satan can detect when the adversary has set a target against a leader. This is especially true when the secular media begin reporting information on a conflict in a major ministry or a local church. I have read articles, with pictures included, that painted a negative picture of a minster. I personally knew the minister and the details of the situation, and the article was completely incorrect, filled with innuendoes and false information. Some would read the same article and completely lose confidence in the minister by believing everything that was written.

Over the years Christians in America have discerned that the secular media—by and large—are anti-Christian, and their focus is on discrediting anyone with a voice to speak to the nation. When an unbelieving journalist reports, most believers say, "That journalist is liberal and biased, and I don't trust what he or she is saying." However, the perception changes if a journalist quotes negative information from former church staff members and those who were on the "inside" of the church or ministry.

The voice of a fellow church member or a fellow believer, adding his or her own "insight" into a collection of allegations, tends to increase the credibility of the report much more than a person who is looking in from the outside. It is common to protect the source by saying, "According to a source who wishes to remain anonymous" or "According to a source who asked not to be identified." Despite the fact that the source is not named, people will accept what is said as fact when it could be a total lie. If an individual is willing to release inside information, but does not want his or her name mentioned, it reveals that person is willing to hurt someone as long as his or her involvement is kept covered. On the Internet people type in their critical comments using a fake name, or they send letters of rebuke without signing their names. I have a nice wastebasket those e-mails and letters go into. If you're not willing to back up your word with your name, then I don't have the time to read what you wrote. When Christians condemn other Christians, it destroys the integrity and reputation of another.

Some time back our ministry hosted a Reformation Movement, drawing more than eight hundred people, mostly youth, in attendance. One woman minister who oversees a small congregation in Arkansas brought her youth group of about eight kids. These youth were all from a Baptist background, and the Lord baptized them in the Holy Spirit during the meeting. After the meeting she said, "I almost missed out on experiencing this blessing this weekend." She continued, "I listen to a minister on the radio, and he was preaching against you, calling you and other ministers 'heretics.' He was saying things that didn't ring true in my spirit, because I had watched you preach on television. I felt the man was either jealous or bitter, so I went ahead and brought the youth, and look at what the Lord has done!"

If this man who was cutting me down was a Bible-hating atheist, no Christian in his right mind would listen to the sewage spewing from his mouth. However, because this man had been in ministry for years and had a following, this added credibility to his assault. Thankfully the Holy Spirit can discern the intent of the heart and expose such foolishness committed in Christ's name. When this same minister is criticized for his statements and negative comments, he becomes defensive and often cuts people off. Funny how goats can dish it out but can't take it!

Goats in the flock will easily expose themselves with their conversations. There is *the intimidator,* who comes to the pastor and says, "I disagree with what you are teaching, and if you don't stop, my family and I are going to quit supporting the church." The *manipulator* comes along and disregards the type of music being sung, reminding the worship leader that he had better get back to singing the old hymns because he will see a lot of people leave the choir if he doesn't. The *dominator goat* is the older man who's been in the church longer than anyone else and feels he has certain privileges others do not. He dominates conversations by reminding folks that he is the oldest member there, he has seen pastors come and go, and he will be in charge no matter who thinks otherwise. An *instigator goat* is the person who detests the pastor and his family and will organize an uprising, just as Korah did against Moses in Numbers 16, reminding the leadership that they are the family with authority. A minister must know his calling and must stand against all forms of manipulation and intimidation.

The Sin of Ministers Attacking Ministers

In the body of Christ there are doctrinal differences, or various opinions such as the type of music or worship, which often separate denominations. However, we can all agree to disagree on those subjects that have no bearing upon our salvation, justification, and eternal destiny. The Word of God must never be used as a weapon against other men of God. I have heard of men using the message of the Cross to assault other followers of Christ and exalt their own ministry since they are the only ones "telling it like it is." Paul preached that the Cross brings salvation and deliverance and was never intended to be a beating stick to crack the skulls of other believers. Paul preached Christ crucified and spoke of his own flesh being crucified, but he never hung his ministry companions upon a cross. A self-righteous Pharisee will wound others, but a true Christian will seek out the wounded and pour in the healing balm.

God's Word is like a sword, but it must never be turned upon a fellow brother or sister. The Word is a rock, but it must never be used to stone someone who has failed. The Word is also a hammer, but it is not intended to serve as the tool to crucify believers on your cross of doctrinal opinions. The Word is water that is intended to refresh, but it should never be the weapon used to drown out the voice of someone you disagree with. The Word is a fire that God Himself uses to purge iniquity from a person, but it is not intended to be used by a fire-handling Christian who wants to burn someone's hide by quoting verses in hate and bitterness.

> If someone says, "I love God," and hates his brother, he is a liar; for he who does not love his brother whom he has seen, how can he love God whom he has not seen? And this commandment we have from Him: that he who loves God must love his brother also.
>
> —1 JOHN 4:20–21

Though I speak with the tongues of men and of angels, but have not love, I have become sounding brass or a clanging cymbal. And though I have the gift of prophecy, and understand all mysteries and all knowledge, and though I have all faith, so that I could remove mountains, but have not love, I am nothing. And though I bestow all my goods to feed the poor, and though I give my body to be burned, but have not love, it profits me nothing.

—1 CORINTHIANS 13:1–3

And whenever you stand praying, if you have anything against anyone, forgive him, that your Father in heaven may also forgive you your trespasses. But if you do not forgive, neither will your Father in heaven forgive your trespasses.

—MARK 11:25–26

Why did Christ say, "Whenever you stand praying…forgive." In Christ's day all forms of prayer by the men in the synagogues and at the temple were offered when standing up. Also, you may not always remember your negative words or bad attitudes expressed during discussions or divisions caused by your actions, but when you stand in the presence of God, the Holy Spirit will often remind you (convict you) of your thoughts, words, and actions. Thus when you "stand praying," the presence of God exposes your own actions to you, causing you to make a choice of either ignoring the prodding of the Spirit or of following through with right actions. To release others through forgiveness is not an option but a *divine instruction*. Forgiving others is not just beneficial in this life, but it is the clear path that leads you to eternal peace.

I believe that the worst manner of death for anyone is to depart this world with unforgiveness by not forgiving others.

As an illustration, years ago I was preparing for a business meeting with leaders of a secular company who dealt with the aged and those near the point of death. My host that day was a Christian woman familiar with my ministry, and we discussed the numerous people she had been near when they had departed this life. She stated that most of the elderly were believers who peacefully departed in a quiet setting with family members at their bedside. However, there had been one departure she had never forgotten.

She stated to me, "A woman was brought to us and placed in a room, and she was one of the most difficult and verbally abusing women I have ever encountered. On two occasions I felt impressed to speak to her about her personal relationship with God. She would curse and defy God's name and say she wanted nothing to do with God. She was bitter and filled with anger and unforgiveness. I was so burdened for her, but I could not penetrate the hatred in her heart. On this particular day she was at the point of her death, and it happened."

When I asked what happened, she replied, "This woman suddenly began to yell out so loudly that her words were disturbing the other patients in their rooms. She began speaking of her feet being on fire and said the fire began moving up her legs. Our nurses ran down the hall shutting the doors to hopefully prevent others from hearing. I watched her die screaming with her eyes opened and in some type of torment. I hope I never see anything like this again."

If unforgiveness can prevent your prayers from being heard, your financial blessing from being released, and your own sins from being forgiven (Matt. 6:12–15; Mark 11:25–26), then you should make amends long before lying on your deathbed! Whether you are a shepherd (minister), a sheep (individual believer), or a goat (an opinionated and self-serving person), no person either departed or living is worth you departing this life with unforgiveness, thereby risking your own eternal destiny. Remember, forgiveness happens on this side of the grave—not in the afterlife.

Chapter 4

WHO IS SITTING IN
YOUR THIRD CHAIR?

O
N SEVERAL OCCASIONS I have used the following illustration. I ask for three chairs, all the same color, shape, and
size, and I place them side by side in a single row. Moving
from left to right, I identify them as the first chair, second chair,
and the third chair. The three represent the three separate sacred
chambers of the tabernacle and the Jewish temple—the first
chair being the *outer court*, the second chair the *inner court*, and
the third chair represents the *holy of holies*. Using three chairs, I
offer an explanation as to why men and women become hurt by
others—they allow the wrong person in the wrong chair.

THREE LEVELS OF PEOPLE

These three chairs are also used to illustrate the three levels of
people you will encounter in life—workers, associations, and
personal. Scripture identifies them in three categories: *hirelings,
servants,* and *friends.* There are three different scriptures related
to these three terms.

A hireling

> I am the good shepherd. The good shepherd gives His life for the sheep. But a hireling, he who is not the shepherd, one who does not own the sheep, sees the wolf coming and leaves the sheep and flees; and the wolf catches the sheep and scatters them. The hireling flees because he is a hireling and does not care about the sheep.
>
> —JOHN 10:11–13

The Greek word for "hireling" found here in John 10:12 is *misthotos*; it refers to a "wage earner." The hireling was someone hired from outside of the family to assist the farmer or rancher by working for a set amount of pay. The danger is that hirelings only work for pay and not out of concern and love for the sheep. The hireling may be with you today and *move on* to some other rancher next week. When a hireling sees the wolf approaching, he flees for his own life instead of protecting the sheep he was assigned to protect.

From a practical perspective a hireling can be what is termed a *church hopper*, someone who travels from one church to the other, setting up camp for a season, until he finds a better opportunity to "use his gifts" and "release his anointing." Their stays in each congregation or ministry are very brief, and their true personalities are concealed with discontent, especially when any form of trouble ensues in their presence. A hireling will always want to first know what is in it for him, not what he can do for the kingdom. I have seen this type of attitude emerge among musicians and singers in a local church. The hireling's motto is: "If you pay, I can play." At times a hireling may be necessary in the early stages until a *called* individual links with the ministry.

A servant

It was Christ who said:

> Who then is a faithful and wise servant, whom his master
> made ruler over his household, to give them food in due
> season? Blessed is that servant whom his master, when he
> comes, will find so doing.
> —MATTHEW 24:45–46

The common Greek word for "servant" is *doulos* and refers to a slave or a servant who involuntarily (is owned by a master) or voluntarily (by personal choice) serves the master. A servant serves his master either by force or out of willingness. While growing up in a minister's home, we had no *choice* as to whether we would attend church three times a week (twice on Sunday and once on Wednesday), and also every night during the protracted weeklong revivals. All of our complaining, excuses of needing to do homework, and "Mom, I think I feel sick" did nothing to prevent us from getting dressed and driving as a family to the services. We were *forced* to obey. However, as a teenager I encountered a life-changing spiritual experience with God, and my outlook was no longer "I have to go to church." It became "I can't wait to get to the church." It was a voluntary action with no resistance.

Today we don't speak of *servants*, as in America the term reminds us of the history of slavery. We speak of *helpers, servers, workers,* and *volunteers.* However, these four terms seem to have one thing in common: they refer to individuals who are willing to serve and work in the church or ministry without asking for any type of financial remuneration in return. No ministry can fulfill its assignments without the assistance of caring individuals who volunteer their time because of their love for Christ and love for the ministry (or church), including their desire to bless others. These are the true *servants* of the Lord. In our own ministry there are more than twenty-five individuals whom Pam and I have known for many years whom we trust and who assist us throughout the year in duplicating the CDs and DVDs in conferences, overseeing the resource tables, and serving as security, ushers, and other necessary positions. The majority of these caring individuals pay their own way and expenses and serve in a professional manner, just as if they were paid staff.

Which chair would you place each level of individuals in? The hireling should remain in the first chair, but the servant should sit in the second chair. When relating this to the ancient Jewish temple, the common Israelite was only permitted in the outer court (symbol of the first chair). The Levites were permitted in both the outer and the inner courts (second chair), but only the high priest was allowed in the holy of holies (the third chair). The outer court was where the common people met to ceremonially wash and offer their sacrifices to God. A hireling can eventually become unstable and cause difficulty in the ministry or church, because when things do not go as he wishes, he will create his own following and leave the local ministry, or he will depart suddenly without any explanation because it is *all about him* and not about loving the sheep and caring for the needs of the flock.

However, in the inner court is where true *fellowship* with the Father occurs. The Greek word for "fellowship" is *koinonia*, a word indicating "mutual participation in an event or those forming a partnership." In the inner court is the table of showbread where we break the bread of the Word together, under the light of the golden menorah, which in the ancient temple represented the manifestations and illumination of the Holy Spirit.

Together we stand at the golden altar making intercession as we pour the incense of our prayers out before God. This is where the servants of the Lord meet together in the second chamber of the house of God, fellowshipping with the Father.

There is only one weakness in being a servant, according to Christ.

> You are My friends if you do whatever I command you. No longer do I call you servants, for a servant does not know what his master is doing; but I have called you friends, for all things that I heard from My Father I have made known to you.
>
> —John 15:14–15

The hireling hangs around for personal gain and for his own benefit. The servant is available to serve because of the love for the sheep and the shepherd. Christ revealed that a servant does not know what the master is doing, which, when paraphrased, indicates that *the servants are not involved with the inner circle decisions of the master.* Servants are not always told the secrets that only close family members know. Just as a hireling will often split the scene when the first sign of trouble arises in the church or ministry, some people who serve can become offended with the ministry leadership if they are not allowed in the inner-circle conversations or inner-circle fellowship session. When not being invited to the dinner at the house, the special fellowship times, or special events and occasions, they too can become offended and eventually turn on the leadership, departing in offense instead of smiling and continuing to work their assignment.

A friend

After several years of spending day and night with His chosen disciples, Christ informed them He was advancing them or, as we would say, "bumping them up" from servants to friends. The Greek word for "friends" here is *philos,* from the Greek word commonly translated as "love," and refers to someone who is greatly beloved. A *friend* in this context is not just a common acquaintance as when we use the phrase "This is a friend of mine," but in the context it is a more affectionate type of love. It includes the concept of loyalty to friends, family, and community. The Greek word *philia* identifies the type of love that a family has toward one another.

Servants who are loyal are second chair, or inner court people. However, there are some servants whose friendships eventually mature into a closer, family-like affection and strong love, and these are repositioned from the second chair into the third chair. The third chair is for the closest of friends and represents the third and most important chamber, the holy of holies, in the Jewish temple. The high priest alone was permitted in this third chamber once a year when God Himself descended into the holy of holies on the Day of Atonement. The high priest made atonement for himself, the priests, and the common people. This chamber was the most intimate of the three, and only a specifically assigned person was permitted in this sacred room. This third chamber, the holy of holies or most holy place, was exclusively reserved for face-to-face, one-on-one encounters between the high priest and God.

The metaphor of the third chair is important, *as not everyone should be permitted in the third chair* of *personal relationships.* This is one of the often overlooked reasons why believers experience hurt, disappointment, and betrayal at times: we allow a first-chair person to advance and be privy to conversations or sensitive personal information while sitting in the third chair. A hireling in a third chair is too immature to handle what he sees or hears and eventually causes harm to himself and others by betraying trusts. A hireling whose hidden agenda is to get close to someone for his own self-serving purposes can become disappointed and cause great distress. How many times have you befriended a person, and as your friendship matures, you begin to confide in that person, sharing confidential information, only to be betrayed when he or she falls out with you and begins revealing the private information against you as a weapon that holds you emotionally hostage. The Word of God is metaphorically called the "sword of the Spirit" (Eph. 6:17). However, the sword of the Word should never be used as a weapon to stab and wound other believers.

There have been occasions when I was in a room with numerous friends of the ministry, and someone would begin to discuss an important yet personal issue. At times I would ask the larger group to excuse themselves for a moment. A *hireling* would immediately complain behind my back, saying, "They don't think I'm good enough to sit in that room with them." The *servant* may say, "Wonder why he asked us to leave? Oh, well, it's none of my business." A *friend* however, will lead the group out and say, "Let's go have lunch while they are talking so we can get back and finish working."

Concerning ministry work, many people have a preconceived idea concerning working in a ministry. This may sound humorous, but there are some men and women who believe that after I arrive at work, I sit in a room praying in the Spirit all day, receiving revelation and inspiration. This is because they only see or know me in a pulpit or conference setting. At times someone will come to work for me with this concept, only to discover that for eight hours they must answer busy phones, take phone orders, pray for individual needs, deal with a few people with a goat attitude on the phone, and actually work! When workers become slack or ineffective, they are required to meet with Pam, who assumes the business meetings and meetings with department heads of the VOE and OCI staff. I released her to assume this responsibility after realizing she was more patient and understanding in dealing with the "sheep cares" on staff.

Everyone needs true friends. However, not all friends are the right type of friends you need when you are needing a close friend. Notice Proverbs 18:24:

A man who has friends must himself be friendly,
But there is a friend who sticks closer than a brother.

There are two different Hebrew words here for the word for "friends" and "friend." The word for "friends" is *rea'*, which is a close companion or an associate, similar to someone you work with or a neighbor. The word for "friend" is a different Hebrew word; this word is *'ahab*, a more intimate word, meaning a friend who has great affection for you. This same Hebrew word, *'ahab*, is used in 2 Chronicles 20:7, where it is written that Abraham was God's "friend," and in Isaiah 41:8, where Abraham is called God's "friend." Thus, the first word is used for an associate, a colleague, and close friend who is a coworker; but the second word is more of a covenant partner, someone who has your back and truly cares for you. The proverb indicates that if you are a friendly person, you will make friends. However, among your lifetime friends, there will only emerge a handful who will become true covenant friends, defending you and never allowing anyone to speak evil of you. These are the ones who *have your back*.

Face-to-Face,
Shoulder-to-Shoulder,
and Back-to-Back

Just as there are three chairs comparable to the three chambers in the tabernacle and Jewish temple, there are three different levels of friendship we experience in any ministry or church. These three can be identified as *face-to-face, shoulder-to-shoulder,* and *back-to-back*. The face-to-face group are first-chair people who are outer-court friends. The shoulder-to-shoulder friends enjoy the second chair—a more personal relationship—and are parallel to inner-court people. The back-to-back relationships become our third-seat friends and our intimate holy-of-holies relationships.

Face-to-face

The face-to-face relationships are the common relationships forged in most local churches. As we enter the congregation each Sunday morning, we see the physical face of fellow members and recognize, "That is Brother or Sister So and So." This is name-face recognition. We may know personal information as to where they work, their personal needs, or burdens they are carrying as we meet in the church lobby face-to-face, shake hands, and say, "God bless you," or "Good to see you!" When we exit the service, we give them a see-you-later handshake and do not see them usually until we return for the next service. These face-to-face meetings seldom emerge from a casual conversation to personal friendships, as each person respects the other's privacy. We worship with people each Sunday whom we never engage in conversation or fellowship with in a more intimate and personal manner, as we are all too busy in life to deal with other people's problems—so we think.

Shoulder-to-shoulder

The second level is shoulder-to-shoulder. When we speak of standing shoulder-to-shoulder with another person, we visualize a picture of two people lifting a load upon their shoulders. When others join with me in the work of the ministry, we are standing shoulder-to-shoulder to help bear together the burdens and weights of God's work. Jesus always sent His disciples forth in pairs—two by two (Luke 10:1). The practical reason was that two working together can encourage one another:

> Two are better than one,
> Because they have a good reward for their labor.
> For if they fall, one will lift up his companion.
> But woe to him who is alone when he falls,
> For he has no one to help him up.
> —ECCLESIASTES 4:9–10

The second possible reason for teaming in twos is penned by Solomon, when he revealed how two working together forms a protection against attack:

> Though one may be overpowered by another, two can
> withstand him.
> And a threefold cord is not quickly broken.
> —ECCLESIASTES 4:12

Two are always better than one. When God formed Adam, He said, "It is not good that man should be alone" (Gen. 2:18). In Hebrew, "alone" in this verse is the word *bad*. The word *alone* means to be separate or be by yourself. "Bad" things can happen when you are living like a loner without someone to encourage you, as you will struggle more mentally when alone. It was when Jacob was alone that he "wrestled" a man to the breaking of day

(Gen. 32:24). When Elijah was alone, he battled depression and requested God to take his life (1 Kings 19:4, 9–10). God created you for friendship and companionship, not for you to isolate yourself and carry your own burdens. We are to "bear one another's burdens" (Gal. 6:2) and pray one for another (James 5:16). When my shoulders are weighed down, I need faithful friends and ministry partners to help lift the burden. These burden bearers are the second-chair servants who are willing to stand in the gap with you and finished the assignments.

Back-to-back

The third level of relationship, and especially important in time of battle, are the *back-to-back* friends. Perhaps you have seen movies showing Roman gladiators who were teamed together in twos, fighting off numerous armed men who were attacking them in the arena. Each warrior can clearly see the enemy directly in front of them, but no one has eyes in his back. Thus the gladiator would grasp the hand or wrist of his fellow warrior, whose back is up against his. As long as he could feel the hand of his battle partner, or his back against his, he knew his *back was covered*, and he could concentrate on the enemy before him.

A Sad but True Story

This story was related to me by a personal friend of the minister it involves. For forty years this minister had pastored mostly small, rural congregations in a southern state. He willingly served as a volunteer in all regional state meetings, parking cars, sweeping floors, and handing out brochures during church conventions. Because of his long tenure in the state, he was viewed as a noble and upright man.

As he entered his sixties, his wife of many years had a nervous breakdown and required hospitalization. The cares of life, pressure of the sickness, and cares of the church had dragged him down emotionally and mentally. Three days a week he bathed her while she babbled incoherent words. As a teen before his conversion, he battled a smoking habit but had stopped at age twenty-one. One night, in total despondence, he left the hospital at three in the morning. He stopped by a convenience store and bought a pack of cigarettes for the first time in forty years. A church member drove by and saw him exiting the store with the cigarettes in his hand. But instead of calling him and checking on his mental state, the member reported the incident to a local pastor.

Instead of following biblical protocol and meeting face-to-face with this brother in the Lord (Matt. 18:15–17), this minister (who actually desired to become pastor of this man's church), in order to *catch him* smoking, dressed in a deer hunter's outfit and hid in the woods near the preacher's house with a camera, filming him as he walked onto the outside deck smoking. The "spy" then drove to the head denominational office and showed the state bishop the film. The result? The denominational leadership immediately threw the man out of his church and removed him from the ministry, without considering his wife or his own emotional and spiritual condition, and they gave the church to the minister sneaking around in the woods. After forty years, and one fleshly failure, the man was cast out like dirty bathwater.

Why is it important to have a close friend watch your back? Because even good people can fail! Noah spent about a hundred years preparing the ark, then following the Flood he was found lying naked and drunk in his tent. Lot was considered a "righteous man" (2 Pet. 2:7–8), yet after fleeing Sodom he was made drunk, impregnating his two daughters, who gave birth to two sons through their father's drunken act. Moses was told to speak to the rock; however, he struck the rock, preventing him from entering the Promised Land. Gideon led three hundred men to battle, defeating the Midianites, and later used a gold offering to build a golden ephod that became an idol. Samson took the gates off a city and torched the fields of the Philistines with three hundred foxes, and yet one woman did more damage than a roaring lion and a thousand Philistines. David was a man after God's own heart, yet his heart was seduced by another man's wife, and an adulterous affair led to a pregnancy and the murder of the husband. God appeared to Solomon twice, and the king constructed the grandest temple in history, only to marry strange women and turn his heart away from God.

The reaction of Noah's sons to their father's drunkenness reveals the *face-to-face* and *back-to-back* reactions. When Noah was drunk in his tent, Ham saw Noah's nakedness and ran to tell his brothers, Shem and Japeth. These two sons refused to look upon their father in this weak condition, instead taking a cloth and covering him. What Ham saw *face-to-face* he was willing to expose to others. Hirelings and outer-court people have no reason to restore a brother and thus "cover a multitude of sins" (James 5:20). Relationships can be built only upon common agreement or agreement combined with love for the person, forming a friendship from the relationship. A third-chair friend will never justify evil or disobedience, but he will never use knowledge to backstab or bring more wounds to an already wounded soul.

Whom Do You Love More?

After many years in ministry I have learned that there is a difference between the love people have for the *ministry* and the love they have for the *minister and his family*. Those who love the minister and his family tend to be individuals or families who were converted to Christ or whose lives were transformed by the preaching and teaching ministry of the man or woman of God. For example, my strongest and most loyal partners are those who were converted to Christ, baptized in the Holy Spirit, or received a definite spiritual awakening through the ministry of the Word. There are occasionally, however, some who will latch on to a ministry, hoping to either be seen and recognized by others, or to eventually make their way into a position of authority. I learned this many years ago when several individuals hooked up with our ministry and served by volunteering. There was one main problem—I began slowly losing good people who no longer wanted to serve the ministry. I discovered that one of these volunteers was running everyone off with a negative attitude and comments.

If you truly love the ministry more than the minister and his family, then when there is a transition in the methods used or a change in the staff, you will possibly become offended. As ministry personnel change and ideas shift among staff, or if the style of music or methods of ministry at the altar change, then you will find yourself frustrated, because they are changing what you love about the ministry. If you love the minister, however, and you have confidence in his or her decisions, then you may not always like changes, but you will remain in your third chair as a friend of the ministry. As Proverbs 17:17 states, "A friend loves at all times."

JESUS HAD THREE GROUPS IN HIS MINISTRY

We can divide the ministry teams of Christ into three groups. There were seventy men sent out in pairs, two by two (Luke 10:1). However, there were twelve personally selected disciples traveling full-time as part of the traveling evangelistic team. Within these twelve men there was also an *inner circle* of three: Peter, James, and John. During the most important moments in Christ's life, these men were separated out from among the other nine men and invited to sit in the *third chair* of intimate friendship. Peter, James, and John were at the Transfiguration (Matt. 17:1–5) and near to Christ in the Garden of Gethsemane where His sweat became as blood (Mark 14:32–33). These three would experience the *glory* of the Transfiguration and the *gore* of the agony of Christ sweating blood.

I have often wondered why these three were chosen above the others. The answer was in preparation for their future ministries. After Pentecost we see where Peter became the apostle to the circumcised. James became a leader in the early church before his beheading in Acts 12, and church history reveals that John led the church after the apostle's death and penned the great vision of the Apocalypse from the island of Patmos.

You must exercise *discernment* when permitting a person to step from your outer circle of friends into your inner circle. Individuals with a hireling nature who are moved from the outer court to the inner court tend to be those who will initiate the betrayals of trust, using what they know to enhance their ego and build their own importance in their eyes and in the eyes of others who will *ooh and ahh* with their inside information. Also remember that hirelings will not be long-term people in a church or a ministry, as they are known to be unsettled in their spirits and rather *free spirits*, roaming from place to place to find people to affirm and bless them.

LAZARUS—
AVOIDING THE STINK

Biblical stories often hold a literal narrative, yet concealed within the text are practical spiritual principles that can apply to present-day circumstances. In John chapter 11 Lazarus had died, and Christ purposely delayed four days before journeying to the graveyard. In Christ's time the bodies were not embalmed but were buried the same day of their death by wrapping the corpse in linen and placing the body in a limestone niche, rolling a large stone over the opening. These tombs were called "sepulchres" (Matt. 23:27, KJV). The spiritual application is that we believers keep all of our stinking past and stinking present covered up and hidden from others. The stone over the tomb was not to keep Lazarus secure, because dead things can't get up. It was to keep outsiders from getting in.

When Jesus arrived, He demanded the men to remove the stone. The concern with the religious folks was the stink that would emerge from the grave once the covering concealing the dead was removed. Was Jesus trying to "stir up a stink" by removing the stone? All the foul odors were in the tomb, and none was on the outside. The people were basically saying, "We would rather have this man out of sight and smell rather than have to deal with his stinking situation."

On occasion noted ministers who pastor a living, thriving congregation with a growing ministry are suddenly stricken with a satanic-inspired dart that wounds them to the point of spiritual death. They lose their church, their ministry, their influence, and friends. They find themselves like Lazarus, bound up in death clothes and laid aside from public ministry by religious folks who roll a stone over them and walk away, leaving them to rot by themselves while their closest family and friends stand aside watching and weeping.

Know this: Jesus is not afraid of your stinking circumstances! Perhaps there are things in your life or a terrible secret in your family that is too painful for you to deal with. You have thrown it away, covering it up, but every day you have to pass the "tomb" and be reminded of the secret—just like the parents whose child was killed in an automobile accident. Each day they must drive to work on the same road, twice a day going and coming, and passing the intersection where their child was killed. The sorrow and pain sting each time they pass the site. Burying Lazarus does not remove the *memories* of Lazarus. Is the "stink" that covered your life incest, abuse, a personal bondage, or a person who sexually molested you as a child?

REMOVING THE STONE

Lazarus needed a new life, and the large round stone was hindering him from getting out and experiencing freedom. Removing the stone was not intended to release the unpleasant smell of death, but it was intended for Lazarus to get up, step out of his past, and drop the grave clothes of bondage holding him down. In Lazarus's case, they already knew his circumstances and his past. He was sick, he had died, he was in grave clothes, and he was stinking.

Here is the odd part of the story. Once the stone was removed and Lazarus came forth being loosed from his linen bandages, no one said anything else about the stink! This always amazed me, until I realized that when Christ takes you from death to life, He removes your stinking past, never to bring it up again! The past was forgotten when the resurrection power of Christ was released on this corpse. Christ got him up and got him out!

RESTORING THE LAZARUSES IN MINISTRY

Lazarus is also a story of restoration. After he was raised from the dead, a group of religious people secretly threatened to kill him! I have seen ministers fall into sin, end up like Lazarus with a stink, get back, and be restored, only to have a small group of self-righteous ministers criticizing the restoration process and talking about the stink from the past instead of the resurrection of the present. There are some who are "buffet believers," picking and choosing verses that fit their personal theological opinions and using the Bible as a rock to throw at weaker brothers. This can be true with how some ministers present the message of the Cross. This message should never be used as a weapon to beat up other believers with whom a fellow minister disagrees. The true message of the Cross is forgiveness, reconciliation, and restoration. Paul wrote:

> Brethren, if a man is overtaken in any trespass, you who are spiritual restore such a one in a spirit of gentleness, considering yourself lest you also be tempted. Bear one another's burdens, and so fulfill the law of Christ.
>
> —GALATIANS 6:1–2

The Greek word for "overtaken" here is *prolambano* and means, "to take in advance." Literally it means to "forestall the less-favored person at a social meal." Figuratively it means to anticipate or to be surprised. In this reference it means to be suddenly overwhelmed and caught off guard by a trespass. The Greek philosopher, historian, and geographer Strabo used this word related to a rhinoceros that, in a contest with an elephant, suddenly rips into the belly of the elephant, preventing the elephant from using its trunk to stop the assault. The word was also used in ancient Greece to describe a vessel that is whirled by the waves and suddenly dashed on the rocks. The idea in Paul's instruction was that when a believer is blindsided and suddenly finds himself in a sin situation and suddenly falls. All men and women will experience temptation. However there is a difference between falling into a temptation and premeditating sin after long seasons of temptation.

Paul taught that fellow believers should "restore" those who are overtaken. The Greek word for "restore" is used as a metaphor to fix a dislocated limb through the hands of a skilled physician.[1] If a man broke his leg, the doctor would not say, "Just wrap a cloth around it and lie in bed for a few weeks." If the broken bone is not properly reset, the man may eventually lose his leg, at worse, or have a terrible limp for life at the least. In either case, the loss of the limb could have been prevented with proper care. Just as a broken bone takes time to be restored to strength, when a believer falls into sin and needs restoration, it requires time to heal emotionally and spiritually.

I grew up in a very traditional and conservative denomination. In the early years I can recall times in which ministers would fall into a serious sin or some form of immorality. Immediately if the investigation proved guilt, the minister's license was revoked, he was removed from the pulpit for one to three years, and he was cut off from any form of ministry until he went through a *restoration process*. In some cases the minister had been faithful for many years, and a one-time failure was the only negative mark against him. At other times it was revealed that the problem was a consistent lifestyle—however, both were disciplined in the same manner despite that in one instance the minister may have been *overtaken*, and in the other the minister was *practicing a lifestyle* of inappropriate behavior. When the punishment was meted out, I often felt that some ministers continued to punish a person who was already at the lowest moment of his or her life—discouraged, defeated, and despondent.

What was called *restoration* in the early days of many full gospel movements often had very little *restoring* in the process. The man and his family were outcast, treated like lepers, and unwelcomed in church denominational conventions; whispers were passed along when he or his family walked into the building. Restoring a person in no way places approval on the act of disobedience or smooths over the hurt. But we are told to treat fallen believers with meekness, lest we should also be overtaken in the same fault.

KILLING TRUST

Trust must be built on a foundation of mutual love and respect. As your relationships with others blossom, you will begin to appreciate their strengths and see their weaknesses. Often in ministry, when people begin to see a weakness in attitude or of the flesh in someone else, they lessen their respect and somehow equate the weakness with hypocrisy.

As an example, some of the greatest men and women of God have dealt with a temper. A person can become angry and yet do not sin (Eph. 4:26). Christ turned in anger upon the money changers' tables in the temple, as the original intent of the temple was a "house of prayer" (Matt. 21:13). In this instance His anger was justified, as a sacred place was being corrupted for personal gain. As an opposite example, King Uzziah infringed upon the office of the high priest by offering incense on the golden altar. Only a chosen priest could perform this duty. The Bible indicates, "But when he was strong his heart was lifted up, to his destruction, for he transgressed against the LORD his God by entering the temple of the LORD to burn incense on the altar of incense" (2 Chron. 26:16). Instead of repenting, we read:

> Then Uzziah became furious; and he had a censer in his hand to burn incense. And while he was angry with the priests, leprosy broke out on his forehead, before the priests in the house of the LORD, beside the incense altar. And Azariah the chief priest and all the priests looked at him, and there, on his forehead, he was leprous; so they thrust him out of that place. Indeed he also hurried to get out, because the LORD had struck him.
>
> —2 CHRONICLES 26:19–20

Uzziah did a right thing in a wrong way. Offering incense was required for the prayers of the people to ascend to God in heaven (Exod. 30:7–8; Ps. 141:2). As judgment for his actions, Uzziah became a leper. He was cut off as king and lived in an "isolated house" until his death (2 Chron. 26:21).

The problem with anger is that when it manifests, it has a *cutting off* and *isolating* effect. When Moses was told to speak to the rock, but in his frustration with the people he became angry and struck the rock, at that moment he forfeited his future inheritance because God forbid him to enter the Promised Land (Num. 20:8–12). When Cain slew Abel in jealousy, he was sent into the land of Nod, a word that means wandering (Gen. 4:16). The reason anger, especially an unrestrained temper, is so destructive is because no one wants to be around a person who is angry all the time.

It has been discovered that when a person becomes extremely angry, not only does it increase the heartbeat and breathing rate and raise the blood pressure, but also a major, verbal outburst shuts down the immune system for a period of about six hours.[2] I know of adults who were raised around a father or mother with a violent temper, causing harassment through verbal abuse, and the mental images are replayed in their minds to this day. Solomon instructed:

> Make no friendship with an angry man,
> And with a furious man do not go,
> Lest you learn his ways
> And set a snare for your soul.
> —PROVERBS 22:24–25

More wrong choices are made when *anger* is the root reason for the decision. When King Saul was in battle, Israel was chasing the Philistines when Saul said, "And the men of Israel were distressed that day, for Saul had placed the people under oath, saying, 'Cursed is the man who eats any food until evening, before I have taken vengeance on my enemies.' So none of the people tasted food" (1 Sam. 14:24). Soldiers, when under the stress of war, must eat to retain strength, and this decision was made because there was *confusion* among the Israelites and the men were "distressed" (1 Sam. 14:19, 24). The Bible says, "The people were faint" (v. 28). When the battle ended, the men were so hungry they slaughtered animals on the ground and ate them with blood, something forbidden in the Law of Moses (Lev. 7:26;

1 Sam. 14:33). Your wrong decision will always impact those closest to you. Just as the wrong words of Saul caused the people to eat the wrong things, your negative words in anger will cause the words from the mouth of others to produce *blood*—not of animals, but cutting words like swords that will make people bleed in their minds and hearts.

One of the biggest trust killers is when a marital partner has been proven to be unfaithful to another through adultery. This act is the highest form of betrayal and is the most difficult of any in a marriage to restore trust. *Forgiveness is the only path to restoration.* I have known of couples where one was unfaithful and the innocent companion chose not to forgive, initiating a divorce, only years later to confess, "I reacted in anger and made a mistake by not forgiving and healing." Others choose counseling and willingly forgave, and in many instances bonded with a much stronger relationship, saving their family in the process. Forgiveness is the key to the door of restoring trust, and forgiveness is a choice.

WHO ARE YOUR THIRD-CHAIR FRIENDS?

The fear of failure is one of the greatest hindrances to stepping out in faith. The second is simply fear itself. The most common Greek word in the New Testament for *fear* is *phobos*, whose original meaning was "flight," caused by being frightened or scared. The idea is that fear is something that causes you to flee and produces the emotion of dread, anxiety or terror.[3] When speaking of the "fear of God," the Greek word for "fear" is *eulabeia*, signifying caution or godly reverence. Our relationship with God should not be a *phobia* type of fear, but it should be a reverence toward His greatness, as our relationship is based upon mutual love.

When you have allowed a first-chair hireling to sit in your third chair of intimacy, and as a result you have been betrayed, you will become fearful of *friendship failures* and will create a resistance to new friends, becoming a social recluse in an effort to protect your emotions from another wound. In your mind it is better to have no close friends than to see friendships turn sour or experience a close friend taking on the Judas goat nature and betraying your trust. Imagine that if after His resurrection Christ would have had an inner-circle meeting with the disciples and said, "Our treasurer, Judas, betrayed Me and committed suicide. Peter denied Me, at the same time cursing Me, and Thomas doubted I was alive. All of you ran like scared chickens at My crucifixion, and only John remained loyal. You are the worst friends a man could have. After forty-two months with you I have wasted my time, and I'm going back to heaven. So you're on your own, cause I'm outta here!"

Christ chose twelve common men with clashing personalities, and despite their faults, failures, and fleshly flip-flops, He invested forty-two months into their futures, knowing that the Holy Spirit would empower them to successfully complete their assignments. He was not looking for spiritual perfection but personal obedience. What are you looking for in a third-chair friend—perfection or friendship? I believe God places specific people in your life at specific seasons for certain assignments. The key is being able to discern the motive and motivation that are connecting you with others and to know the people whom you should let into your inner circle. This discernment is sharpened through prayer.

Years ago a man was invited to a local church to give his

"testimony." The fellow said he had served in the Vietnam War and had a rather supernatural story of protection and conversion that bordered on a Saul of Tarsus–type conversion. The tale was so dramatic and impressive that churches booked him for speaking engagements, and eventually word of this dramatic conversion came to the leaders in the denominational headquarters. He was to be invited to speak at the main General Assembly to tens of thousands of people. However, one godly minister felt in his gut that something wasn't right, and he set out to research the story. After digging through the facts, he discovered this man had never served in the military and was making up an elaborate story to play on the emotions of the people. This counterfeit *hireling* was attempting to gain access to the third chair in order to gain credibility for his outrageous story and to merchandise the gospel for his personal benefit.

At age eighteen I was impressed with the testimony of a man who alleged he had been a leading member of the Church of Satan and was miraculously converted, with death threats now hanging over him like a dark cloud. His words were so convincing that he became a popular speaker in youth conferences and special church conventions to warn the youth of the evils of the occult. I had every cassette tape message of his stories that I could acquire, and I would repeat his testimony to others, including the details that had stunned his listeners. My wise father said he felt uneasy when he heard him and believed that something didn't ring true. After some behind-the-scenes research, it was discovered he was a sham and a counterfeit believer, using the gospel for personal gain. This goat was working his way from the outer court to the sacred ministry pulpit, but he was exposed by observant shepherds.

Growing up it was difficult if not impossible for a counterfeit

Christian to blind the eyes of the praying saints. They did not look at the manifestation but at the fruit, not at the swelling words but whether or not the words "bore witness" with the Holy Spirit within them. True believers have the same Spirit, and our spirits will bear witness. The phrase "beareth witness" is found in the King James Version in John 5:32; 8:18; Romans 8:16; and 1 John 5:6, and it means, "to collaborate with evidence or to testify in agreement." The Holy Spirit, through prayer, will collaborate with you about the three levels of *friends* and reveal whom you can trust, those who should remain in the outer court of your life, and those who should be allowed closer access. After all, the Holy Spirit sees and hears actions and words that are done and said in private.

Chapter 5

I HEARD WHAT YOU SAID IN YOUR TENT

THE FASTEST WAY to lose a friend, lose favor with God, and end up sleeping by yourself on the couch is to open your big mouth at the wrong time, wrong place, and with the wrong words! Keep in mind you will never have to apologize for what you never said, or repent of what you never did, or confess what never happened! However, we humans will get in a small room and *discuss* private matters as though no one but our inner circle is listening. This must be how Israel felt in their tents.

> Nevertheless you would not go up, but rebelled against the command of the LORD your God; and you complained in your tents, and said, "Because the LORD hates us, He has brought us out of the land of Egypt to deliver us into the hand of the Amorites, to destroy us."
> —DEUTERONOMY 1:26–27

On the night of Passover all Hebrew firstborn sons were spared from the angel of death. (See Exodus 12.) Israel began an organized exodus into the wilderness, a massive land bridge of sand, dirt, and rock connecting Egypt to their Promised Land. These were ex-slaves, immediately liberated, and they had a *slave mentality* as they pitched their tents in the desert. For decades they had lived in Egyptian *government housing*, and the government provided food. They had no life of their own except a soul tie to a spirit of Egypt. In Egypt they never had to use their faith for any provision or to witness any miracle. It was a rut and a routine, but at least they had government food and housing. That was until they began their journey and realized they were living in a dry place.

Before long the complaints began filtering through the camp. They went something like this:

> And the children of Israel said to them, "Oh, that we had died by the hand of the LORD in the land of Egypt, when we sat by the pots of meat and when we ate bread to the full! For you have brought us out into this wilderness to kill this whole assembly with hunger."
> —EXODUS 16:3

> Now the mixed multitude who were among them yielded to intense craving; so the children of Israel also wept again and said: "Who will give us meat to eat? We remember the fish which we ate freely in Egypt, the cucumbers, the melons, the leeks, the onions, and the garlic; but now our whole being is dried up; there is nothing at all except this manna before our eyes!"
> —NUMBERS 11:4–6

> And the people spoke against God and against Moses: "Why have you brought us up out of Egypt to die in the wilderness? For there is no food and no water, and our soul loathes this worthless bread."
> —NUMBERS 21:5

Their primary problem was their mouths. They wanted the food of Egypt in their mouths, fresh water in their mouths, flesh instead of manna in their mouths, and they used their mouths to complain continually! Their biggest problem was they did not understand the plan and the process of God and how He was actually protecting them from danger. When Israel departed from Egypt, Pharaoh pursued them, for he had lost his entire work base of slaves that was constructing buildings for his empire. He chased Israel with the intent that if they were to see war, they would change their minds and return to Egypt (Exod. 13:17). Normally it would be a two-week journey through coastal areas to get from Egypt to the Promised Land, near Gaza. However, God knew the Philistines, Israel's enemy, had iron weapons, and they dwelt in the coastal areas. The Lord would lead Israel through the land of the weaker children of Ammon and across Jordan to the Golan Heights region.

When the people retired at night in their tents, the murmuring began. The word *murmured* is found ten times in the King James Version of the Old Testament, eight times referring to Israel's negative words in the wilderness (Exod. 15:24; 16:2; 17:3; Num. 14:2, 29; 16:41; Deut. 1:27; Ps. 106:25). Yet there are two different Hebrew words for *murmured* used in those ten passages. One word is *luwn*, from a root word meaning, "to stop or to stay overnight (in a bad sense)." It refers to getting stuck in a bad attitude over one place or one thing. A different word is used in this passage:

> And ye murmured in your tents, and said, Because the LORD hated us, he hath brought us forth out of the land of Egypt, to deliver us into the hand of the Amorites, to destroy us.
>
> —DEUTERONOMY 1:27, KJV

This word *murmured* in Hebrew is *ragan*, and it means, "to grumble, in a sense of rebellion." Murmuring, or as we would say, complaining, begins with a few negative words. However, before long we find ourselves getting stuck on the subject by continually bringing it up. As with Israel, the greatest danger is continual complaining, which will lead to a rebellious attitude and an unteachable spirit.

Believers may speak in secret about other believers; however, the Bible says, "And the LORD heard the sound of your words, and was angry" (Deut. 1:34). When Miriam complained about the wife of Moses, the Lord struck her with leprosy, and she spent seven days isolated, later being healed through Moses's prayer (Num. 12:1–16).

The complaints of the people provoked God, and God responded by sending various plagues and judgments to bring the people to repentance.

May I suggest that if you attend a local church with your children, and there is something in the ministry you are in disagreement with, do not roast the minister, the staff, and the people at your Saturday or Sunday afternoon dinner! We are not spiritual cannibals, and when you chew someone up and then spit them out in front of the tender minds of your children, you are actually planting corrupt seeds of mistrust in your church leadership. As your children mature into teenagers, the seeds will be like an audio CD replaying your conversations and giving them an excuse to avoid church.

When God heard Israel, Moses wrote that God did not only hear their "words" in their tents but He also heard the "voice of your words" (Deut. 1:34, KJV; 5:28, KJV). As I pondered the phrase "voice of your words," I noticed the Hebrew word for "voice" here is *qowl* and means, "aloud, claiming, proclamation, thunder, a voice and to yell." Hearing the "voice of your words" seems to indicate that God heard not only their words but also the *tone* in which they were spoken. I discovered very early in my ministry that it was not always what I said but the *spirit* in which I said it, or, at times, the *tone* in which I expressed myself that was important. Did you ever hear when growing up, "Don't you speak to me in that tone of voice"?

When growing children cause parents to become upset, most parents will initially call their children by their first name and say, "Don't do that." However, if the child persists, the parents tone changes to, "I said, don't do that." If that child continues to ignore his parent's words, most likely he then hears his full name called, such as I did: *"Perry Fred Stone Junior*, I said don't do that, and I mean it!" If you were a male and named after your father, when Momma called you "Junior," it meant that "Senior" was about to be invited into the conflict, and Senior usually wore a big, black leather belt. The voice of your parents' words reflected in the tone was an indicator as to whether there would be *peace* or *conflict* in the near future!

In the wilderness it was not simply words of, "Wow, this is going be a long trip, and I hope I don't get tired of this manna," or "Some T-bone steaks would taste good about now." No, the tone of the average ex-slave-now-Hebrew-traveler indicated anger, disgust, and lack of honor for God's provision. Their tone and negative words provoked God to send them running in circles in a rocky desert for forty years. As with ancient Israel, when being pulled into a conflict, our temperature rises along with our blood pressure, and soon the smooth, soothing words have become a high-pitched shouting match where voices are interrupting one another, and the "voice *within* the words" becomes a sword that divides opinions in the room. Solomon, a man who had much to say about your mouth and your words, wrote, "A soft answer turns away wrath, but a harsh word stirs up anger" (Prov. 15:1).

The tone in your words is motivated by the spirit behind your words. Soft answers reflect a spirit of peace. Silence reflects emotional discipline and a calm spirit. Sudden answers and quick responses before the question is asked often have an underlying spirit of impatience. Anger often has its roots in a form of pride. Christ spoke and said, "The words that I speak to you are spirit, and they are life" (John 6:63). Biblical words contain spiritual authority that transforms you from darkness to light and from death to life.

In the Bible King Uzziah infringed upon the office of the priest by entering the holy place and offering his own personal incense on the altar of incense. Suddenly the priests gathered around him, rebuking him because they understood the spiritual danger of his actions. While the incense chalice was in the king's hand, he became hot with anger and was struck with leprosy (2 Chron. 26:19–20).

When entering God's presence, all worshippers must enter with humility. Uzziah ruled as king of Judah for fifty-two years, thus becoming comfortable with being the sole political authority. After faithfully following the Lord throughout his life, in his later years he had become overly self-confident and apparently believed he was above the laws that others were required to follow. At the temple the incense, when placed upon the golden altar, represented the prayers of thousands of Jews ascending before God. Uzziah demonstrated that spiritual power in the *wrong hands* can be abused, misused, and manipulated to the detriment of the people and the minister.

The second observation is that of *arrogant leadership* in spiritual situations. During his rule Uzziah's name had spread abroad and was made strong (2 Chron. 26:15). However, we read: "But when he was strong his heart was lifted up, to his destruction, for he transgressed against the LORD his God by entering the temple of the LORD to burn incense on the altar of incense" (v. 16). Uzziah felt qualified to fill a position he was unqualified and unanointed to do. His prosperity led to pride, and pride led to his downfall. The God of Israel separated kings from priests, but in nations such as Egypt the king (Pharaoh) was also the spiritual leader of the nation. Perhaps Uzziah felt he deserved total control of political and spiritual matters. At times ministers and spiritual leaders believe they are above the instructions they are teaching others and deserve special fringe benefits of leadership.

After the king had conquered, built, ruled, and dominated, what *thrill* remained for him? His ambition for something new led him to cross a forbidden line. Often, extremely prosperous people become bored with the routine, and the new becomes old and the old becomes boring; thus they seek a new thing, a new experience, a new drug, and often a new wife or husband to fulfill a missing *thrill factor.*

Notice where leprosy struck the rebellious king—not in the hands but in the forehead (2 Chron. 26:19). Leprosy is a spreading disease that eats away parts of the body, leaving the person isolated. The disobedience that was on the king's *mind* was exposed for all to see, and he was forced to resign as king and live apart from his own family and friends—a leper till he died. This demonstrates how thoughts become actions and actions are performed through obedience or disobedience.

Spiritual manipulation in the ministry is as dangerous as outright flagrant sin. Occasionally the sheep are in the pew and the goat is in the pulpit. This is seen in the forms of spiritual manipulation occurring on occasions. This is especially true in relation to tithes, offerings, or financial giving. There are some men who will "prophesy a blessing over you" for a specific amount of money—the larger the offering, the longer the "word from the Lord." These goat ministers are shearing the sheep for their wool and eating the sheep for dinner. Ezekiel warned of these careless shepherds when he wrote:

> And the word of the LORD came to me, saying, "Son of man, prophesy against the shepherds of Israel, prophesy and say to them, 'Thus says the Lord GOD to the shepherds: "Woe to the shepherds of Israel who feed themselves! Should not the shepherds feed the flocks? You eat the fat and clothe yourselves with the wool; you slaughter the fatlings, but you do not feed the flock. The weak you have not strengthened, nor have you healed those who were sick, nor bound up the broken, nor brought back what was driven away, nor sought what was lost; but with force and cruelty you have ruled them. So they were scattered because there was no shepherd."'"
> —EZEKIEL 34:1–5

THE VISION OF
THE WEAK SHEEP

Several years ago a missionary friend experienced a very troubling vision (not a dream, but a vision) of the condition of the sheep within the local church. He was standing on the back side of a huge field observing tens of thousands of sheep grazing in the pasture. On a wooded hill above the field began to appear spiritual leaders from the past, all who had passed on, and they were observing the flock. These flocks were in order, as they had been raised and fed by godly, spiritually minded leaders in the past. The sheep appeared strong, vibrant, and covered with thick, white wool. As these men would speak, the entire flock was united and would stop to hear the instruction. As he began observing more closely, the faces of men from generations past began flashing in and out. The Lord impressed him that in days gone by the church was protected and nourished by men who loved the sheep and protected them with their lives.

Suddenly a new set of faces appeared, and this time greed was in the eyes of several of the shepherds as they fixed their gaze upon the flock and prepared to make a move to use the sheep for personal gain and for their own pleasure. However, they were being restrained by what the missionary could hear were thousands of prayers going up to God. He saw time pass with more shepherds and faces appearing before him, overlooking the field. He saw large buildings and debts begin to increase, and the need for more and more money. The intentions were good, but the sheep were suffering as men began building their own systems using the flock for gain. The sheep were being stripped of their wool, shivering and confused as they became weak and began wandering aimlessly through the field without any clear direction. He saw men beginning to argue over control and the spoil, causing more sheep to become dispersed, discouraged, and disgruntled. The sheep became so weak they were no longer able to lift their heads and felt insecure and unprotected from the dangers surrounding them.

At that moment he heard the voice of several well-known ministers begin to call out for help as other men of God arrived and began to scream out, "These are the last days; they really are." Suddenly the tens of thousands turned to millions of sheep, and they focused their attention on a new mountain with new ministers whose love for the sheep would unite them again for a final move of God's Spirit in the earth!

The condition of many sheep reminds me of Jeremiah's words:

> "Woe to the shepherds who destroy and scatter the sheep of My pasture!" says the LORD. Therefore thus says the LORD God of Israel against the shepherds who feed My people: "You have scattered My flock, driven them away, and not attended to them."
>
> —JEREMIAH 23:1–2

America has tens of thousands of good ministers, but we also have some who are goats in the pulpit! They remind me of the Pharisees in Christ's time who had taken away the "key of knowledge" to control the masses (Luke 11:52). They exalted their own traditions above the Word of God (Mark 7:9–13) and chose form and ritual over the true power of God (Mark 12:24). Prior to the return of Christ the wheat and tares are in the same field (Matt. 13:30); the sheep and goats are in the same pasture (Matt. 25:32), and the good and bad fish are in the same net (Matt. 13:48). A time of separation will come in the future to separate the sheep from goats, the tares from the wheat, and the good fish from the bad fish. Just as the Lord will expose the goats in the flock to the shepherd, we must allow God to expose the goat shepherds to the leadership in the church. As my grandfather used to say: "If a man thinks he is right but is wrong, just give him time and enough rope and he will hang himself."

Christ made it clear in the New Testament that: "For nothing is secret that will not be revealed, nor anything hidden that will not be known and come to light" (Luke 8:17). He also warned, "I say to you that for every idle word men may speak, they will give account of it in the day of judgment" (Matt. 12:36). Idle words are words that are lazy, useless, and of no purpose. They are words that are fruitless and cause barrenness. Perhaps you have heard it said that if you can't say something positive about others, then remain silent and say nothing at all. Always remember, anyone who will talk openly and freely about others in a negative manner will also have you in sight when your name comes up to speak negatively about you. Our instruction in Scripture is to edify (or build up) one another in the faith and not tear down others in unbelief. When our heart is right but our thinking is wrong, or when our thinking is right but our heart is spiritually out of rhythm, our eyes of understanding and manner of thinking will be foggy and can affect our relationships.

Chapter 6

HAVING RIGHT EYES
WITH THE WRONG BRAIN

I**N AN INTERESTING** verse Christ said that the "lamp of the body is the eye" (Matt. 6:22). Years ago I learned that this is more than a metaphor. My wife and I were at the beauty salon of a Christian woman, when she began discussing the fact that the human eye actually revealed what is going in within the body. She said, "Remember how the early doctors would shine a light in your eyes during an examination? When you have a problem in the organs of the body, there is small dot that appears on the pupil of the eye. The round pupil is like a clock, with the numbers one to twelve, and these spots reveal a problem in the body."

Skeptical, I asked her to look into Pam's eyes. She did and replied, "You've had back trouble!" She did not know that Pam had back surgery when she was nineteen! She also looked into my eye and saw a problem that I had been dealing with physically. I was quite amazed. She said, "This fact about the eye was known as far back as the time of the Egyptians, and Christ being the Creator knew that the eye revealed what was going on in the body."

The eye views images that are in turn relayed to the brain, where the brain takes the information stored on the subject the eyes see and, in turn, begins processing a mental impression that *judges* what it has received, what it means, how it effects the viewer, and so many other details. The brain is an amazing creation. Billions of bits of information bombard it every second, and filters in the brain keep it from becoming overloaded. Approximately two thousand bits of information per second enter the brain.[1] Every thought that enters the brain produces a corresponding electrochemical reaction in the brain. Signals from the brain are what releases chemicals—some with positive effects on the body, while others produce negative effects on the organs in the body.

DULL EARS AND DUMB MINDS

It is astonishing how, at times, religious folks hear what they wish, and everything they hear is with a twist. Christ was speaking of the Communion supper when He said believers should eat His flesh and drink His blood to have life (John 6:54). This message sent everyone except the disciples of Christ running out of the synagogue with the thought that Christ was breaking the law, as Moses forbid drinking any form of blood. Christ was using the analogy of His body and predicting they would destroy the temple (His physical body), and in three days He would build it back again (John 2:19). The Jews misread the statement and went around saying Christ said He would destroy the temple building.

When He confronted a Samaritan prostitute at a well, Jesus spoke of water He provided that would satisfy a person, and that person would never thirst again. The woman began asking Christ where His bucket was to get this water. He was speaking spiritually and she was thinking naturally (John 4:6–15). Even when Christ cured the sick on the Sabbath, instead of rejoicing in the miracle, the Pharisees began complaining that Christ healed a man on the Sabbath (Matt. 12:10–12).

These statements and others made Jesus *controversial* to those who misread and misquoted His intent. However, this controversy was not due to Christ actually being controversial, but it was because His statements were *misunderstood* by those who often didn't have spiritual discernment. Jesus identified the problem this way:

> For the hearts of this people have grown dull.
> Their ears are hard of hearing,
> And their eyes they have closed,
> Lest they should see with their eyes and hear with their
>   ears,
> Lest they should understand with their hearts and turn,
> So that I should heal them.
> —MATTHEW 13:15

Eyes can see natural elements, but spiritual eyes represent the ability to properly discern actions. Ears hear natural sounds, but ears are also the gateway into the mind and conscience. Spiritual ears perceive and correctly divide words. Throughout my own ministry I have researched and taught information that was not always known or understood by my listeners. In the mid 1980s I taught a prophetic message titled "The Ashes of the Red Heifer," dealing with the rebuilding of a future Jewish temple. This was one of my most interesting messages, but it became my most criticized one as many people had never heard the subject before and the content was different from the average prophetic word.

During this same season I began teaching on the significance of the Jewish people in their covenants with God, and rumors spread that I was teaching "Dual Covenant Theology." In the late 1980s I began an emphasis on the Hebraic roots of Christianity, including the feasts and the patterns of Christ fulfilling the symbolism and mysteries concealed in the Law. Messianic believers began attending services wearing *tallits*, and occasionally banners, tambourines, and a few shofars appeared at the main conferences. Suddenly it was repeated that I was a *Judaizer* and *pulling people into the Law*. When I began to minister outside of the place of my denominational upbringing, some leaders suggested that pastors refuse to allow me to preach in their pulpits, as I was not a *systems man*! Some of these attitudes were ignorance on steroids, the hijacking of just good old common sense, and in other instances critics gone wild.

Right Eyes
Wrong Brain

We sang a song as a child, "Be careful, little eyes, what you see." I will add, "Be careful, little eyes, what you *think* you see." Your eyes cannot lie, because you saw it, and what you see is fact…right? But your perception of what you saw is not always what you thought you saw. Years ago, after my dad was married, one of his sisters was in the hospital, and he drove his younger sister to the hospital for a visit. It was raining, and after parking the car, Dad held the umbrella over his sister while both of them ran across the road in the direction of the hospital.

Dad was conducting a revival at a church in the area that was going quite well. After this incident, he preached that night with no response from the congregation, and the atmosphere was completely different. This went on for two nights. Finally he asked the pastor what was wrong, and the pastor confessed that one of his men *saw him with a strange woman, hugging her and running across the street trying to keep from being seen!* That night Dad invited two of his sisters to the church, including his youngest. Before preaching, he introduced them and told how one was in a hospital and he had taken his younger sister to the hospital. He stared at the "old goat" in the pew who had started the false story. The man turned red in the face and hung his head! If Dad had not corrected this rumor, it would have spread and damaged his good reputation. The man's eyes were right—Dad was with a young woman, but his brain's interpretation was wrong, as he created his own perception without knowledge, and *perception without knowledge* is the root of false rumors.

Years ago my wife and I sold our house to a missionary for what we had in it and made no profit, as we felt impressed of the Holy Spirit to do so. I told my wife the Lord would bless us for sowing into this family's life. A few weeks later a businessman called and asked me if I would receive a vehicle he would give me. I actually needed a personal vehicle and told him I would receive it. The vehicle was a black Hummer, a vehicle that at that time I did not know I would literally need in the future to drive on the youth ranch property, which has deep ditches and rolling hills.

One day my wife was driving the Hummer in our hometown of Cleveland. Later that day she came to me and said, "You will not believe what someone posted on the Internet." I read the comment from a person who had seen Pam driving the Hummer, and it basically said, "I just saw Pam Stone driving in a new expensive Hummer with her head stuck in the air. I guess she used the money from donations from the widows and poor people who support them!" Of course others were jumping on the bandwagon, disgusted that we would spend ministry money on an expensive vehicle!

My first *fleshly* reaction was to invite my tattooed, ex-druggie, Harley biker on staff to find out who would speak about my dear wife and post such lies and to "bust a few chops!" However, calm prevailed.

Notice the following: the critic had no actual facts, made up his own facts, and wrote out these imaginary facts as real facts. He was ignorant of the *true facts* that God had blessed us for sowing into the life of a missionary, and ignorant that the vehicle was a free gift and no money exchanged hands. He was also ignorant of the fact there is not one proud bone in the body of my sweetheart, Pam. It is clear he was also ignorant of the fact that VOE is a 501(c)(3) organization, and we cannot take money from the VOE ministry account and purchase a personal vehicle. In fact, I cannot drive a ministry vehicle for personal use; I must use them only for ministry trips or personally pay for the usage. Had this precious businessman not given us this vehicle, I was going to be required to purchase a personal vehicle just to travel to our office and back, as the IRS has strict regulations placed on not-for-profits.

The same is true concerning my ministry books, CDs, DVDs, and any resource material produced and paid for by the VOE. I have read blogs of how "much money Perry Stone is personally making" through the sales of his resource materials on television. Once again, as my father used to say, "This is ignorance gone to roost!" I legally cannot and do not receive one single penny from any resource book, DVD, or CD offered on television, in the *Voice of Evangelism* magazine, or at the resource table at our conferences. All income from anything I have written or recorded goes 100 percent into the VOE ministry. As an additional note, the VOE and OCI (Omega Center International) do not personally belong to me or Pam or any family member; they are under the voting power of a Board of Directors of very godly men whose decisions are final in the business matters, including *our salaries and benefits,* of which we have no voting power or input concerning. All income received must be used for the purpose of ministry and ministry-related outreaches, including the salaries and insurance for about twenty-five full-time and four part-time workers.

Those marking their opinions as facts are actually lying and are in spiritual danger for spreading information of which they are wrong.

I am convinced that individuals making such uninformed statements do so not in the interest of information, but in the selfish desire of giving a voice to their own internal, murky mixture of animosity, jealousy, or even hatred. Solomon wrote of the evil man who speaks "froward things" (Prov. 2:12, KJV). The Hebrew word *froward* can refer to something that is a fraud, or false. In English the word *froward* is used for someone not willing to comply with what is reasonable, someone stubborn and contrary. Thus, those who out of stubbornness and pride make judgmental statements without true knowledge are operating in some form of evil and arrogant intent. Paul wrote, "Therefore judge nothing before the time, until the Lord comes, who will both bring to light the hidden things of darkness and reveal the counsels of the hearts" (1 Cor. 4:5).

The brain is the hard drive computer for the entire body. But Christ taught that the "light of the body is the eye" (Luke 11:34, KJV). I like the way the Amplified explains this unique statement:

Your eye is the lamp of your body; when your eye (your conscience) is sound and fulfilling its office, your whole body is full of light; but when it is not sound and is not fulfilling its office, your body is full of darkness.

—LUKE 11:34, AMP

What you see enters your brain, where the conscience is the seat of the emotional part of the brain. If what you see, discern, or perceive with your eyes is correctly understood, then light—illumination and understanding—will fill your mind. If, however, what you see forges a false imagination, your own self-interpretations, or your own twisted perception, then it will impact the mind. The mind controls the rest of the body, including what you will say with your mouth.

For example, let's show you a picture of someone you have never met or seen. It is the picture of child about ten years of age, and all you see in this picture is a very large stomach—nothing else—no face, arms, or legs, just a ten-year-old with a big belly. If I say, "What about this kid?", some may suggest, "It looks like he needs to go on a diet and has been eating too much!" You would really feel bad after I revealed to you the entire picture and the picture was actually the bloated belly of a starving ten-year-old in a foreign nation. You saw one part—the belly—without seeing the *whole picture*, and you judged what you saw without complete information. It is literally impossible to set a conclusion without *all* of the facts. This is why, when an alleged criminal is arrested, that person is "innocent until proven guilty." You cannot convict on opinion but only on evidence. Sadly, many opinions are formed by what *others tell us* and not from our own personal information.

Throughout my ministry, friends and partners have invited friends or family to a major conference or a one-night meeting in their area, only to hear, "I've heard some negative things about him!"

They ask, "Have you ever read a book, listened to a tape, or heard him on television?"

Usually the answer is, "No." But they can tell you about their mother's sister, who has a daughter, whose father knew someone who heard me preach! One time my youth pastor, Mark Casto, was working out at the YMCA in Cleveland. He and another friend were talking about the ministry. Suddenly a man in the gym spoke up and yelled, "Perry Stone is a heretic!" The man had never read a book, been in a meeting, or heard a tape, but he was certain my teaching was heretical. About that time Mark received a word of knowledge and said to the man, "You have the same spirit of [he named a radio and television minister], and you have taken on this preacher's negative, bad spirit because he can't stand Perry's ministry!" The man turned red and hung his head. He admitted that this television minister was his "pastor" (even though he lived ten hours away). His opinion was formed by his listening to a critic and not by any facts.

RIGHT BRAIN
BUT WRONG EYES

Believers are to continually renew their minds by the washing of the water of the Word (Eph. 5:26). Paul wrote to Titus of the "washing of regeneration and renewing of the Holy Spirit" (Titus 3:5). The Greek word for *regeneration* means "to renovate something that is old." When we restore a house, we remove the broken, insect-infested wood, fill in the cracks, and repaint the walls! It is somewhat of an enigma that a believer can have the right mind and at times the wrong eyes. One of the three categories that all sin falls into is the "lust of the eyes."

The first biblical example of this was when the serpent tempted Eve to eat of the tree of the knowledge of good and evil. Eve "saw that the tree was good" (Gen. 3:6). The irony of this scene is that God had personally created all of the trees in the garden, and even God said that "everything that He had made...was very good" (Gen. 1:31). The tree of the knowledge of good and evil was a forbidden tree to eat, just as there are plants (including some mushrooms) that were created by the Lord that would kill if a human eats from them. God created the rattlesnake and the copperhead for a purpose, but humans had better hope they are never bitten by one!

Eve saw this tree continually, as it was in the midst of the garden near the tree of life. However, there was never any interest in eating the fruit until the serpent had Eve focus her eyes upon the fruit, and she began to *lust* with her eyes. Her mind was well informed, and through Adam she knew God's warning that eating would result in death. But instead of passing by the tree as she had done on so many occasions, she began *focusing upon the forbidden*, and she and Adam were unable to resist the temptation to "be like God" (Gen 3:5).

Believers who have the right thinking but the wrong eyes can fall into various temptations and eventually sin. This *eye factor* is especially true with men as it relates to the opposite sex. The chemical reactions within the male reproductive system are stimulated by sight, whereas women are stimulated by words or touch. This is why most pornography is geared to men. Strip clubs have women dancing and men watching. The eye is the door into the soul and the spirit, as what we see stirs either positive or negative emotions. This explains how men of God who minister the Word and walk a good walk of faith at times will fall into a sexual sin. Their minds held the seed of the Word, but their eyes were slowly dimmed, and their blurred focus altered their reasoning. Perhaps this is why Peter wrote:

> …having eyes full of adultery and that cannot cease from sin, enticing unstable souls. They have a heart trained in covetous practices, and are accursed children.
>
> —2 PETER 2:14

Men as far back as Job understood the importance of *eye protection* as to what the eyes see, which enters the heart. Job wrote:

> I have made a covenant with my eyes;
> Why then should I look upon a young woman?
>
> —JOB 31:1

We can have a right eye by guarding what we see and still have wrong thinking. We can also have the correct information and the good seed firmly planted in the mind, but if we are undisciplined with our eyes, then continually focusing upon the forbidden will eventually break our resistance and cause us to sin. Wrong thinking combined with wrong seeing is what leads to unfounded rumors that can at times damage the reputation of a person.

WHEN RUMORS COST LIVES

The apostle Paul penned fourteen letters that were later compiled in the New Testament Canon. Paul was physically abused and verbally falsely accused from outside enemies until the final two years of his ministry. After arriving in Rome, he ministered two years in his own house unhindered (Acts 28:30–31). Then, in AD 64, the emperor of Rome, Nero, in response to a conflict with his Senate, plotted and initiated a fire in Rome that began in Circus Maximus and burned nearly all of the city.[2] To escape the wrath of the Senate and the people, Nero conveniently blamed the fire on the Christians, effectively linking Paul to a secret Roman rebellion and accusing him of being behind these fires. Later, Nero appeased the angry Romans by beheading Paul. Paul wrote his last epistle to Timothy, saying:

> This you know, that all those in Asia have turned away from me, among whom are Phygellus and Hermogenes. The Lord grant mercy to the household of Onesiphorus, for he often refreshed me, and was not ashamed of my chain; but when he arrived in Rome, he sought me out very zealously and found me.
>
> —2 TIMOTHY 1:15–17

Paul spent many years converting thousands, starting churches, and ministering throughout Asia. For many years these Gentile congregations loved and prayed for Paul. However, as the rumor spread that Paul directed a Roman rebellion by attempting to burn Rome to the ground, word traveled through the Roman territories and came to the ears of the churches, including Paul's friends and converts. This totally false rumor caused "all of Asia" to turn from Paul, losing confidence in his ministry, and becoming ashamed of him for being locked up in prison. Just like the case of Joseph, a wrong accusation placed an innocent man behind bars. The rumor was a lie, the perception was incorrect, and the truth was not realized until after Paul's beheading when history revealed the details of Nero's conspiracy against Rome and Paul. This apostle gave his life, being beaten, imprisoned, stoned, and persecuted for the gospel (2 Cor. 11:22–28). When Paul arrived at the conclusion of his life and ministry, in the final seven verses in his final epistle he wrote these words:

> At my first defense no one stood with me, but all forsook
> me. May it not be charged against them.
>
> —2 Timothy 4:16

Paul's strength was in the Lord, who had delivered him from the mouth of the lion, and Paul was still believing at this crisis moment that God could deliver him from the evil workers conspiring against him. (See 2 Timothy 4:16–18.) This narrative proves that *false rumors* can not only kill a person's reputation but also literally cost the person his life. When Christ was standing trial, His false accusers could find nothing illegal to accuse Him with. Suddenly a false accuser spoke up and repeated a statement Christ made, saying the temple would be destroyed in three days and He would build it back again. The *temple* was a metaphor of Christ's body (a temple of the Holy Spirit, 1 Cor. 3:16); revealing that He would be dead for three days and would be raised on the third day (John 2:19). Christ's statement became twisted, repeated without the original intent, and used to bring a judgment of death to Him for threatening the temple (Matt. 26:59–65).

John wrote, "Do not judge according to appearance, but judge with righteous judgment" (John 7:24). We are also told that, "Man looks at the outward appearance, but the Lord looks at the heart" (1 Sam. 16:7). I have met individuals who look like they couldn't rub two pennies together, yet later I found out they were millionaires. I have seen others dressed to the hilt and looking as though they walked out of a *Glamour* magazine, looking like a millionaire, but it was all an outward show. I have seen men

whose appearance and countenance looked intimidating out-
wardly, but inwardly they were some of the most gentle and com-
passionate to the needs of others. I have also observed a quiet
man become a raging lion.

As an illustration of an incorrect "appearance judgment,"
years ago I asked my wife to appear on a closing program of the
Manna-fest telecast. She was very tired but reluctantly agreed,
and we did a closing together. A few days later we received an
e-mail from a woman who was rebuking Pam for not "looking
happy," and she even commented on her appearance.

I responded to the e-mail informing the woman of something she "didn't know," which was that Pam had just experienced a miscarriage, was somewhat sick and not feeling well,
and was quite sad. My wife had every right not be excited and
smiling. I firmly rebuked this person for judging by *appearance*
without *knowledge*.

While the Scripture defers judgment to God, believers are
required to discern truth and not be deceived by false doctrine.
We are also assigned to inspect the spiritual fruit that is present
or missing from the life of a fellow believer. Christ taught, "By
their fruits you will know them," teaching us that a good tree
can't produce bad fruit and a corrupt tree cannot produce good
fruit (Matt. 7:17–20). And Paul emphasized the importance of
love when he wrote:

> Though I speak with the tongues of men and of angels, but
> have not love, I have become sounding brass or a clanging
> cymbal. And though I have the gift of prophecy, and under-
> stand all mysteries and all knowledge, and though I have
> all faith, so that I could remove mountains, but have not
> love, I am nothing. And though I bestow all my goods to

feed the poor, and though I give my body to be burned, but have not love, it profits me nothing.

—1 Corinthians 13:1–3

Spiritual fruit grows from a tree rooted in love and not from a ground scorched with criticism. Unless we walk in love, our works are in vain and our spiritual manifestations are useless. This includes our worship. If love motivates our worship, God receives it. If worship is performance only, it is accepted by men but rejected by the Lord, as true worshippers must worship "in spirit and truth" (John 4:24). It is sad to say, but in a local congregation, at times, the worship team, including singers and musicians, are the one target of the adversary, who uses pride, jealousy, and a competitive spirit to disrupt the flow of the Spirit.

Chapter 7

WHEN SATAN FELL FROM HEAVEN, HE LANDED IN MY CHOIR

MANY YEARS AGO I was ministering at Free Chapel Worship Center in Gainesville, Georgia, pastored by Jentezen Franklin, my close friend of many years. From the time Jentezen became pastor in Gainesville, I was one of his main evangelists each year, and I have watched the church grow from their first building with 350 people to the new facility with about 8,000 or more attending each Sunday. The church's ministry of music and worship is noted throughout the region. However, in that earlier season there was a major shifting in the leadership, which was creating a serious challenge.

I call these moments "the dueling worship leaders," where obviously one was trying to out-sing, out-worship, and out-praise the other! It was then that Jentezen said one of the funniest statements, one I am certain pastors have often thought. He said, "When Satan fell from heaven, I think he must have landed in my choir!" He then asked, "Why is it that there seems to be more issues out of the music department than any other ministry in the church?"

It seems that the most talented people are often the most sensitive with their emotions in a ministry. The subtle attack of the enemy often brews contention, jealousy, and darts of division in one of the most important aspects of ministry—the ministry of music and worship. To the biblically informed believer, it comes as no surprise that the ministry of music is one area that must continually be guarded from the adversary. When we read Ezekiel 28 and Isaiah 14, the biblical prophets indicate that Lucifer (or Satan) was originally an anointed cherub whom God created with special built-in abilities to create sound and music.

Our second observation is that worship is the main spiritual activity in heaven, and it never ceases. Angels have no rest day or night as they stand before God's throne saying, "Holy, holy, holy, Lord God Almighty" (Rev. 4:8). When earthly time eventually collides with eternity and ceases to exist, worship will be hosted by angels and resurrected saints for ages upon ages.

Heaven's Ambush

In 2 Chronicles 20:21–22, singing set an ambush against Israel's enemies:

> And when he had consulted with the people, he appointed those who should sing to the LORD, and who should praise the beauty of holiness, as they went out before the army and were saying: "Praise the LORD, for His mercy endures forever." Now when they began to sing and to praise, the LORD set ambushes against the people of Ammon, Moab, and Mount Seir, who had come against Judah; and they were defeated.

The power of music can create an atmosphere or a special mood. For example, you never sing "O Little Town of Bethlehem" on the Fourth of July, as the music does not fit the season. Playing "The Star-Spangled Banner" on Christmas morning would seem strange and even out of place. Specific songs are geared to special seasons. You don't sing "Happy Birthday" at a funeral! Music is not only seasonal, but it also creates emotion. This is witnessed when the bride, in her white flowing gown, enters the doors of the sanctuary and the church organist begins playing the tune of the famous wedding march. Reality suddenly hits the mom, but especially the father of the bride, as often he fights back tears. When seeing our troops and hearing the classic "God Bless America," I am moved greatly by emotion as I recall the sacrifice of men and women of the armed forces.

The third fact is very important, and that is that songs recall memories. Years ago at my Partner's Conference I preached a message called, "Someone Give Me Back My Brain," in which I discussed the various aspects of the brain in relation to our temptations and struggles in life.

The one aspect covered that started quite a discussion was why old people tend to find a comfort zone in the church, circle the wagons, and often spend precious time complaining about things that amount to nothing more than opinions, not worth spending time arguing about. The pew is too hard, the building is too cold, the PA system is too loud, and then there is the music! There is more contention concerning the style or instruments linked with the music in a church than any other one single issue.

I have ministered in thousands of churches and have pondered the question as to why there is such division and confusion over the music issue. Some people like only hymns, and others the red-backed hymnal. Some suggest God only listens to Southern Gospel, and still others feel that bluegrass is the only road to heaven. The youth want a more *contemporary* sound, and the middle-aged enjoy the praise and worship music being sung globally in conferences and conventions.

When we are younger, we want to be a little older. When we are six, we are almost seven. When we are twelve, we will be fifteen before long and get a start on our driver's license. At sixteen we want to be eighteen, and some at eighteen can't wait until they are twenty-one. Then we turn fifty. We brag on this *milestone*, but in reality it feels like a *millstone* around our neck that indicates we are not the spring chickens we once were and things are about to change. It is at this age that something neurological occurs in the brain:

> Neuroimaging has shown that as we age, the center of cognitive gravity tends to shift from the imaginative right brain to the logical left brain. And this neurological tendency presents a grave spiritual danger. At some point, most of us stop living out of imagination [or vision and dreaming] and start living out of memory. Instead of living by faith, we live by logic. Instead of going after our dreams, we stop circling Jericho.[1]

This natural process is very revealing. The older we get, the more we tend to revert back to our younger days, including the type of music we grew up with. This is why Bill Gaither has been extremely successful in producing millions of CDs and DVDs with old gospel songs. If you observe Bill's audience, you see that the majority is over fifty and were raised in church where these songs were sung. Each song has a specific memory attached to it.

This is the amazing link between songs and memories. If I asked you to remember a specific sermon you heard at a specific place in the early 1970s, you may recall one or two, or you may not recall any. However, when you hear a song, you can often recall the place you were and the people around you as you tap into the memory.

Memory is a good thing if we are not hindering the future by dwelling in the past. In fact, when King David was in crisis, he often looked into the pages of Israel's past history, recalling the goodness and miracles of the Lord on behalf of His chosen people. However, when we demand that "our music" must be the music in the church, then we are missing the very reasons for music in the church. Is it our desire to be entertained and have someone swoon into a microphone creating tiny goose bumps on our arms and a feel-good feeling as we reminisce of an old country church or a large gospel tent? There is certainly a time for basking in the joyful memories of early days, but worship is not about *us*; it is about *God*.

NO IRON IN GOD'S HOUSE

In the prophetic scriptures iron was a metal associated with the ancient Roman Empire. (See Daniel 2.) The beast in Daniel 7 had "iron teeth" that devoured and broke others in pieces (v. 7). The metal iron symbolizes war, fighting, strength, and violence. In the ancient Roman Empire iron was forged into armor and weapons of war. God instructed Israel to build altars out of natural stone, and not to use iron to cut the rock or shape them man's way:

And there you shall build an altar to the LORD your God,
an altar of stones; you shall not use an iron tool on them.

—DEUTERONOMY 27:5

Each stone taken from the earth is distinct and unique in size, weight, and color, just as every believer who makes up the body of Christ and approaches the altar of repentance is unique in appearance, strength, and weakness. If iron is a metal symbolizing war, and the altar must be constructed without iron tools, the message is that we must approach God without evil intent and never with a spirit of fighting among the "living stones" that make up the congregation (1 Pet. 2:5).

Centuries later when Solomon was constructing the temple in Jerusalem, he used beautiful white limestone when building God's House. We read:

And the temple, when it was being built, was built with stone finished at the quarry, so that no hammer or chisel or any iron tool was heard in the temple while it was being built.

—1 KINGS 6:7

The spiritual application here is clear. The temple would be the house of God, the center of the feasts, new moons, and Sabbaths. *Jerusalem*, the city of the temple is called in Hebrew *Yerushalayim*, which means, "city of peace." Solomon's (who built the first permanent Jewish temple in Jerusalem) name in Hebrew is *Sholomo* and is related to the Hebrew word *shalom*, meaning "peace." Thus the emphasis of the temple and Jerusalem was to be a place where God's peace ruled and manifested among the worshippers at His house. Just as iron and clay cannot cling to one another (Dan. 2:43), worship and warfare cannot exist in the same house. Solomon precut the stones from a huge rock quarry, and workers brought them on large carts to Mount Moriah where they were laid in their proper settings. The confused noise of chisels banging against limestone ashlars was forbidden on the holy mount.

Have you ever considered the conversations entering the Lord's ears when He watches all of his "living stones" who form that holy nation called *the church* (1 Pet. 2:5) assemble in His house? Between the sound system, the lights, the temperature, the seating arrangements, and the type of music, iron begins slapping against the stones, creating confusion and contention. One pastor told me that after each Sunday morning service about ten of the same people come to him complaining about something they did not like or enjoy about the service. He said he understands why God became so fed up that He chose to slay the adults who came out of Egypt, preventing them from inheriting the Promised Land!

Now back to the choir. The power of music cannot be underestimated, even in a church setting. Here is my observation after years of ministry.

1. Music breaks all *religious barriers* in the sense that people may not enjoy any form of preaching, but all people enjoy some style of music.

2. Second, music carries an *emotional response*, especially when used in a secular film. The type of music joined with the setting causes people to cry or to have an emotional response based on the mixture of the acting, the scene, and the music. This is why millions of dollars are spent on the musical arrangements of major motion pictures; the musical

scores can also become number one hits, creating more income.

3. Music is also *international,* as all nations have their own form of music and special instruments that are distinct to their religion or their culture.

4. Music carries *influence*, as seen with such men as Elvis Presley, who is still one of the number-one selling musical artists years after his death.

Knowing the power of music, is it any wonder that the adversary attempts to bring division into the church through the styles or types of music? I always warn believers not to become critical of the choir, the style, or even the types of instruments used in a service, especially since the Book of Psalms indicates all forms of instruments are acceptable in worship if they are set aside for the worship of the Almighty.

After years of ministry experience I am certain that it is possible for a believer to prematurely abort a spiritual breakthrough after prayer if they begin to speak contrary words to the prayers they have prayed. The spirit world is moved by words (Dan. 10:12). We cannot be "double-minded" (James 1:8) and say today, "God, I believe You for this," and then next week confess, "I don't know what God is doing; He is not hearing me, and I'm tired of it." Remember that unbelief will always cancel out faith (Matt. 13:54–58), and true faith will also crush unbelief (Mark 9:14–29). It is the faith in your heart and confession of your mouth that seals your salvation (Rom. 10:10). Maintaining a positive confession in the Word of God may at times seem contradictory to your circumstances; however, seizing onto your confession will become the anchor that holds your ship as the storms are erupting in the ocean of your life. At times these storms take the form of moral attacks on believers. What must we do when a minister of the gospel has failed and fallen in the midst of the battles? We will explore this in the next chapter.

Chapter 8

BELIEVERS WHO ARE VEXED BY A DEVIL

I N MATTHEW 15 Christ departed from His normal ministry circuit to travel north along the coast of two cities: Tyre and Sidon, located near Lebanon, a strong, pagan Gentile area. However, a Canaanite woman must have heard of Christ's ministry, as she addressed Him "Son of David," a phrase devout Jews knew was attached to their Messiah, who would descend from the tribal lineage of King David. Her petition was not for herself but for her daughter, who was "vexed with a devil."

> And, behold, a woman of Canaan came out of the same coasts, and cried unto him, saying, Have mercy on me, O Lord, thou Son of David; my daughter is grievously vexed with a devil.
>
> —MATTHEW 15:22, KJV

In the New Testament there are three distinct words identifying the work of a devil, or a demon, in a person's life.

1. The strongest level of control is *demonic possession*, from the Greek word *daimonizomai*, meaning, "to be possessed or totally controlled by a demon."

2. The 1611 King James Version uses the word *devil* sixty-one times, from the Greek word *diabolos*, meaning "an accuser or a slanderer." The devil is a proper name given to Satan (Luke 4:2–6); however, the word is also used of individual evil, foul, and unclean spirits (Matt. 9:32; 12:22; Luke 8:29). There is one devil but many individual devils under Satan's direct authority.

3. Among the ancient Greeks a *daimon* was an inferior deity, either good or bad. Some suggest the meaning of *daimon* is derived from the root *da*, meaning, "a knowing one."[1]

When an individual is "possessed," that person loses self-control and is like a puppet on a string, fulfilling the thoughts and desires of the demon possessing him or her. One of the most graphic descriptions of a possessed person is the man of Gadara in Mark 5, who is tormented to the point that he cannot sleep at night and is cutting himself, perhaps being driven by the demon to attempt suicide. He is crying out loudly in torment. Men are unable to physically restrain him, and the community is fearful of him (vv. 1–9). He is possessed with a spirit called "Legion." This name was actually a word used to identify a large cohort of Roman soldiers, who in that day were divided into groups, the largest being a Roman legion of between five thousand and six thousand men. The word *legion* comes from the Latin *legio*, meaning, "a levy." During the first three centuries the Roman army had between twenty-five to thirty-four legions.[2] It was the tenth legion of Rome that eventually surrounded and destroyed Jerusalem in AD 70.

When the unclean spirits were expelled from the man, they

entered two thousand swine, and the swine reacted immediately by running violently into the sea and drowning. This suggests that the spirit of this one man was being inhabited by two thousand evil spirits. His life was in ruins, his mind was tormented, his body was being abused, and he was dwelling in a graveyard, a place of death and memories. When Christ stepped into the graveyard, the tormented man was liberated and freed to get out of the graveyard!

Demon possession is the highest level of bondage. The second form of attack is demonic oppression. Acts 10:38 says, "How God anointed Jesus of Nazareth with the Holy Spirit and with power, who went about doing good and healing all who were oppressed by the devil, for God was with Him." The word *oppress* in Greek means "to exercise power over." Demon possession is when the spirit dwells in the human spirit. Demon oppression can be a control of the spirit, but it is more a control of the mind and thought process. Being oppressed of a devil is described as having a tight band around your mind in which you cannot think clearly, or it is described by those who have experienced it as a feeling of hopelessness, darkness, and despair.

In the Matthew 15 narrative, a woman's daughter was "grievously vexed" of a devil. In Luke 6:18, many people were "vexed" with unclean spirits. This word *vexed* here is *ochleo*, and it means "to disturb or trouble or harass."[3] This *vexation* can be spiritual, mental, or physical, as each human consists of a body (physical), soul (mind), and spirit (1 Thess. 5:23). If it is physical, the unclean spirit can be a *spirit of infirmity*, whose presence causes sickness in your life (Luke 13:11–13). If the attack is mental, the attack will impact your thinking, creating negative and depressing thoughts. From a spiritual perspective, spirits are assigned to keep individuals away from the light and truth of the gospel.

The reason for revealing the various forms of spiritual, mental, or physical harassment is to understand that both believers and unbelievers can come under the attacks of vexation and oppression of evil spirits. This is significant when dealing with the subject of unforgiveness in the life of a believer.

In Christ's revelation of the parable of the unforgiving servant, when the king heard that the servant he had forgiven of a huge debt refused to forgive and release his fellow servant from a small debt, the king was angry and had the unforgiving servant arrested and placed in prison until he not only learned how to forgive but also actually did forgive.

> And his master was angry, and delivered him to the torturers until he should pay all that was due to him. So My heavenly Father also will do to you if each of you, from his heart, does not forgive his brother his trespasses.
> —MATTHEW 18:34–35

The King James Version says the man was delivered to the "tormentors." In the setting when this was taught, the people hearing Christ would have understood the meaning of turning a person over to the "tormentors." In the harshest sense, a tormentor, or torturer, was a man within the prison who would use whips or whatever was necessary to get the truth from the person receiving the beating. This could be accomplished by placing a person on a rack, or in stocks, and beating him until he confessed of a crime or revealed the information being demanded. In the New Testament this particular Greek word used for "tormentors," which is *basanistes*, is only used in Matthew 18.

Remember the context of the story in Matthew 18. A servant forgiven by the king refuses to forgive a fellow worker. The unforgiving man is delivered to the tormentor, until he pays for the error of his ways. Here is one way I believe that an unforgiving person can experience such actions taken against them: when a Bible-believing Christian refuses to walk in the knowledge of releasing others, that person can forfeit the protective covering of his or her own spiritual hedge.

UNFORGIVENESS REMOVES HEDGES

In the Book of Job God surrounded Job, his property, and his family with a "hedge" that prevented any form of evil or satanic spirits from penetrating his health, wealth, and family. When the hedge was temporarily lifted, Job lost his wealth, health, and family. Job was upright, feared God, shunned evil, and did nothing wrong to invite this attack. However, notice what caused the hedge to return.

During Job's trial three men (with another joining later) came to Job with their philosophical and spiritual reasons as to why he had lost everything. Finally God Himself intervened and told the three friends of Job they did not speak the right thing to Him and to bring Job an offering to offer and they would be forgiven (Job 42:7–9). The next verse is quite revealing:

> And the LORD restored Job's losses when he prayed for his friends. Indeed the LORD gave Job twice as much as he had before.
> —JOB 42:10

For several months Job's friends had spoken words that were filled with personal opinions, wrong observations, and incorrect interpretations of events. Instead of Job attempting to retaliate against them, sending them home and refusing to speak, he sat in the dust and countered their false claims with facts. When the

Almighty exposed these friends, Job did not speak out and say, "I knew I was right and you were wrong. I guess God really spoke to you, didn't He?" Instead Job placed a sacrifice on the altar for his friends and began to pray for them. Immediately the hedge that had been removed was reset and a double portion was restored to him!

Based on numerous examples and Scripture, much emphasis is placed upon your words and how you treat others. The misuse of words and the verbal behind-the-scene abuse leveled at other believers can eventually initiate a satanic attack by removing the hedge-like protection surrounding you. One tree should not produce two opposite forms of fruit, and from one fountain should not flow sweet and salt water; from the same mouth should not come blessing and cursing (James 3:10–14). While this *double standard* should not exist in a believer, it does within many. Some members of churches will sing, cry, and worship in the choir, then sit at a restaurant on Sunday afternoon and complain about the worship leader, the musicians, the praise team, and the type of songs being sung. In his epistle James speaks more about the tongue and words than any other single New Testament writer. He suggests, "Let your 'Yes,' be 'Yes,' and your 'No,' 'No,'" lest we fall into condemnation (James 5:12).

The reason words are so powerful and dangerous at times is that by our words we can be either justified or condemned (Matt. 12:37). When police arrest an alleged criminal, he is read his or her Miranda rights and told, "Anything that you say or do may be used against you in the court of law." The judgment determined by actions and words either justify and set free the person, or his actions and words will condemn him and place him in prison. Our own words and actions are viewed by the heavenly judge, God Almighty, in the same manner.

David wrote one of the most important psalms concerning how words can actually be used as weapons of destruction, speaking of secret plots against the righteous:

> Hide me from the secret plots of the wicked,
> From the rebellion of the workers of iniquity,
> Who sharpen their tongue like a sword,
> And bend their bows to shoot their arrows—bitter words,
> That they may shoot in secret at the blameless;
> Suddenly they shoot at him and do not fear.
>
> —Psalm 64:2–4

The tongue of the just is like silver (Prov. 10:20). It is written, "A word fitly spoken is like apples of gold in settings of silver" (Prov. 25:11). On the contrary, the tongue that speaks hateful and negative words is like a sword and, when spoken, is an arrow carrying bitter words. When believers begin forming negative opinions of other believers, they move into the arena of being a judge, which creates a judgmental spirit. Once the believer moves from viewing another believer as a brother or sister in Christ to becoming a judge, then the judge becomes an "accuser of the brethren" (Rev. 12:10). Believers are not assigned to be God's watchdogs over the body of Christ and to go around biting everyone they don't agree with, and neither are they to become the judge, jury, and prosecutor.

Notice that the present positions of both Christ and the Holy Spirit are those of a defense attorney and not a prosecutor. Christ is our "Advocate" with God (1 John 2:1). The Greek word for "advocate" is *parakletos*, which is one called alongside another for help. It was used for a person in a court who was assigned to serve as a counsel for the defense, and one who took a person's case and would plead for them.[4] Christ revealed that He would send the Holy Spirit to us as "another Comforter" (John 14:16, KJV). The word *Comforter* is mentioned four times in the King James Version (John 14:16, 26; 15:26; 16:7). The Greek word for "another" does not mean a different comforter but "another of the same sort."[5] The Greek word for "Comforter" is the same word translated as "advocate" in 1 John 2:1. Thus we have a helper on earth and a helper in heaven who stands alongside of us to help us in our time of sin, weakness, and distress.

Scripture is clear that Christ did not come into the world to condemn the world, but to bring salvation (John 3:17). I believe one of the reasons that Christ warned His followers not to judge others is that what we condemn in others will eventually be found in us! We read:

> Judge not, that you be not judged. For with what judgment you judge, you will be judged; and with the measure you use, it will be measured back to you. And why do you look at the speck in your brother's eye, but do not consider the plank in your own eye?
>
> —MATTHEW 7:1–3

The measure by which a person judges others will be the same measure used against them. This was proved after David secretly sinned against Bathsheba, covering the sin. God exposed the incident to the prophet Nathan, who approached David with a parable of a poor man who had one lamb and a rich man who had many lambs. A traveler was visiting the rich man, and instead of pulling a lamb from his vast reserves, the rich man seized the only lamb of the poor man. Nathan's parable was to see what David's reaction would be. David never realized the parable was his own actions.

David went into a rage and demanded the rich man be

put to death and four lambs restored to the poor man. Nathan announced that David was the man, and that God would spare David's life, but the sword of the Lord would never depart from his house. Shortly after this prediction David's child through Bathsheba was stricken sick and died. Over time David listed a total of four sins through death.

The point is that David, in judging what he thought was a situation involving someone else, was actually meting out his own judgment. David demanded *death* and a fourfold exchange to the rich man in the narrative, yet in turn the death he desired in another was actually passed upon his own house and four sons. The real tragedy here is that when a person has himself committed wrong and seemingly gotten away with it, yet he begins condemning that wrong in others.

As a teenage minister living in Virginia, I can recall how some ministers would become very negative and outspoken when a fellow minister fell into a moral sin and lost his church. However, in some instances it would be revealed years later that the most outspoken and judgmental minister himself was struggling with the same temptation and fell into the same sin as the fallen minister. One man in a large rural church in the mountains of Virginia was so strict that he would measure the hair and dress line of the women singing in the choir, and he spent much time preaching on how women should dress. He was known as the most strict and conservative holiness preacher in the region. Imagine the shock to his church and the community when he ran off with a younger secretary of his church.

This used to puzzle me: "How can they preach against something and then fall into it?" I believe I found a possible answer. When a man is privately struggling with an issue and stands behind a pulpit waxing eloquent in the anointing, he preaches hoping to *deliver himself* from the very thing he is condemning in others. One man confessed this, saying that when he sensed the anointing he felt freedom and would preach more intently with the hopes that the anointing would break the *yoke* in his own life. At times this did occur, and the Holy Spirit actually liberated the person from a possible entrapment that would have devastated his life and ministry. However, it seemed that others did not receive deliverance as they used the pulpit to blast others in a negative manner in order to build up themselves.

One minister, whose actions and sins became nationally known, was an example. At the peak of his ministry he was reaching many nations and people with his television broadcast. He told one group of ministers that he was "the greatest preacher since the apostle Paul" and that he "alone was raised up by the Lord to reach the world." One of his closest friends used to sit at the table eating with this man and his family before the terrible fall of the ministry. Eventually he had to get up and dismiss himself from the table as this man and his family went down the list and began calling names of every known minister, calling them heretics and false prophets, and boasting on their own ministry as the greatest in the world. Yet the sins he preached against were present in his own life. I believe God allowed a protective hedge to be removed from his life and allowed him to experience the same struggles he was judging in others. The ministry of Christ and the Holy Spirit is that of being a *defense attorney*; only Satan is the *prosecutor* or the accuser of the brethren (Rev. 12:10). A prosecutor is designed to attack the accused in an attempt to take information and prove guilt. When you agree with Satan to accuse other believers, then you become a prosecutor to discover guilt, which is NOT a ministry of the Holy Spirit, who convicts a person to bring him or her to repentance to remove guilt.

According to Psalm 64 God will Himself shoot at those who are speaking unjustified, bitter words like arrows toward others who are justified by faith and living for Christ. In the Psalms these individuals will stumble over their own tongues, form their own snares, and end up like Haman and his sons in Persia—hung on the gallows they prepared for others. (See the Book of Esther.)

An example was Peter. When we read Luke's account, we see that Peter was marked for a major shake-up by Satan himself.

There were ten other faithful apostles who could have been targeted, but in this case it was Peter whom Satan desired to sift as wheat (Luke 22:31). I believe the open door to this satanic attack was the sense of *pride* in Peter's words and attitude. He had publicly boasted that if all others denied the Lord, he would never deny Him but would be willing to die with Christ. This was an attitude of spiritual superiority to others and a sense of being better than others.

> But with me it is a very small thing that I should be judged by you or by a human court. In fact, I do not even judge myself. For I know of nothing against myself, yet I am not justified by this; but He who judges me is the Lord. Therefore judge nothing before the time, until the Lord comes, who will both bring to light the hidden things of darkness and reveal the counsels of the hearts.
>
> —1 CORINTHIANS 4:3–5

On one occasion when a well-known minister went on television and cut down in public a fellow minister who had fallen and already repented, following the interview an attorney reminded the accusing minister that he had a few skeletons of his own. I remember this preacher saying, "If you have something, bring it on!" They did know something.

Years ago when Ronald Reagan was president, he had invited the Israeli prime minister to the White House. Reagan had numerous pictures on a table in the Oval Office. The prime minister pointed to a photograph of a known television minister and said, "Who is this man?" Reagan preceded to tell the prime minister that it was a well-known minister with a large following who had stood with him to get elected. The prime minister replied, "Well, he is not who you think he is." Long before anyone had the information that would become public, sources within the intelligence community in Israel were already aware of events taking place.[6]

It would be very unwise for any of us to deal with weakness, temptations, or other issues and become arrogant and proud in our own eyes, condemning others for the same thing we permit in ourselves.

LOSING YOUR HEDGE OF PROTECTION

How does a hedge come down? Satan had to petition God and request for Job's hedge to be removed. However, based on the Psalm 64 warning:

> But God shall shoot at them with an arrow;
> Suddenly they shall be wounded.
> So He will make them stumble over their own tongue;
> All who see them shall flee away.
> —PSALM 64:7–8

Years ago I experienced an open vision of a minister standing in a pulpit preaching, and he was surrounded by a protective hedge that prevented the darts of the enemy from passing into his mind and life. Suddenly he began calling the names of fellow ministers, and as he did, burning arrows began spewing from him. Instead of the arrows landing, however, the burning arrows made a U-turn and went back where they originated from the minister. They began sticking into the hedge, like arrows stuck on a tree. Each time he spoke, calling a minister's name and tearing that person down, another arrow burned his own hedge down. Eventually he was left unprotected, and a snake began crawling toward his feet to bite him. When this concluded, I was reminded of two verses:

> Like a flitting sparrow, like a flying swallow,
> So a curse without cause shall not alight.
> —PROVERBS 26:2

> He who digs a pit will fall into it,
> And whoever breaks through a wall will be bitten by a
> serpent.
> —ECCLESIASTES 10:8

I believe that each believer has some form of a protective hedge or barrier that restrains the adversary from invading our lives at will. In Job's case Satan requested the hedge of covering be removed so he could gain access to Job's personal life, his family, his business, and his health. Job did nothing wrong to initiate a hedge takedown that led to a crisis. However, the psalmist revealed that if words are sent out that are not justified, then the arrows (words) will return to the person sending them, and they will suffer from their own curse that was intended for another person (Ps. 64:1–7). This is the *Haman principle*. Haman secretly prepared ten gallows upon which to hang the Jews. His main opposition was Esther, a Jewish girl who had become queen and had the ear of the king. She exposed his plan, and as I stated previously, Haman and his ten sons were hung by the very ropes they intended to place upon others. (See the Book of Esther.)

The spirit world operates upon certain spiritual laws that are as real and significant as the laws of the land that are legally passed through the judicial branches of our government. If you don't believe these laws exist or are real, then try breaking them! One man "proved" that Americans were not required to pay taxes, as this "law" was passed during a previous war to raise funds during the war; therefore in his interpretation it was no longer valid. He is writing letters today from prison. His opinion of the law had no bearing on his legal defense.[7]

In the spirit realm God has certain laws of the Spirit that operate in both the kingdom of God and the kingdom of Satan. One such law is that God controls life and death. When assaulting Job, Satan was permitted to attack his health, but he could not take his life (Job 2:6). Satan had no power to take the life of Christ, but Christ laid down His life and could pick it up again (John 10:15–18). The adversary made numerous attempts on the life of Paul, but in each case until the time of his departure, Paul escaped from his enemies. In Revelation Christ revealed that He has the "keys of death and hell" (Rev. 1:18), meaning He controls the power of death. Thus, Satan cannot kill a believer who is in covenant with God. However, we must be in the right place with the right people at the right time, and not with the wrong people at the wrong place at the wrong time.

However, there is the one *clause* related to death. Solomon wrote that, "Death and life are in the power of the tongue" (Prov. 18:21). The word for "power" in Hebrew is *yad* and refers to an *open hand* versus a closed one. In other words, you place the power of life and death in your own hand with the words that come out of your mouth! Your mouth and words are a door that is closed when you are silent, but the moment you speak, the door is opened. While Satan has no direct authority to kill a believer, a believer can speak life or, at times, death into his or her own situation, thus opening a door to the enemy.

Closing the Door on Evil Spirits

We think of evil spirits as possessing evil, wicked men or women. However, there are also spirits of infirmity or sickness that can attack a believer. (See Luke 13.) You and I cannot underestimate the power that is released in the spirit world from a legal perspective when a person begins to come into verbal agreement with a bad report. Satan is the accuser of the brethren before God day and night, and, just as in an earthly court, if you agree with the charges against you, then the evidence will be used against you. If I am told I will die in six months and continually say, "Well, folks, this is it.... You know my time is up.... We all have to leave sometime," then I have no *legal authority* to resist the power of death, for I am in agreement with it. If, on the other hand, I am certain that God wills for me to have additional time, then I can act as King Hezekiah did, who was under a death sentence but prayed and was given fifteen more years (2 Kings 20:1–6).

The spirit world operates upon our words that are spoken on earth. Jesus commanded the evil spirits to depart, and they departed; the disciples cast out spirits by their words (Mark 1:23–26; Luke 10:17). In Acts the apostles took dominion of the occult realm by openly commanding spirits to come out of sorcerers, and the evil spirits had no choice but to depart (Acts 16:16–18). We must understand that when we are in agreement with God's written Word, and we are speaking His Word aloud, it is no different than if the Lord Himself were standing beside us speaking the same word—out of our mouths come the phrases that came from God's mouth.

I have observed men or women who would agree with a doctor's negative report and eventually die after prayer. However, those who have been healed have always been those who were not denying the facts but who believed the facts were not the final say-so and that God's healing promises were superior to the death report. Breaking the law gives law enforcement officers the right to arrest a person. Breaking spiritual laws also opens the door to the unwanted assaults of our adversary. One of those spiritual laws that protect us and shut the door is to confess the Word of God and come into agreement with God's Word, as it is written: "Let us hold fast the confession of our hope without wavering, for He who promised is faithful" (Heb. 10:23).

Chapter 9

RESTORING FALLEN MINISTERS
AND CHURCH MEMBERS

EFORE DELVING INTO this very important and, at times,
controversial subject, a little background from me is necessary. I am a fourth-generation minister, with a great-
grandfather, grandfather, and a father who all served as both
traveling evangelists and pastors of local churches. As far back as
the 1930s these four generations, myself included, were linked to
the same denomination—a globally recognized full gospel organization headquartered in Cleveland, Tennessee. Growing up in
a major denomination and beginning an evangelistic ministry at
age eighteen, I have observed advantages and disadvantages of
being linked with one particular organization.

The advantages were ministering in churches where the
believers all held the same doctrinal teachings, the fellowship
and common bond among the ministers, and the structure of
the bishops overseeing local and state congregations and taking
charge of internal conflicts to prevent church splits.

The negative was that some denominational ministers dis-
liked the idea of one of their preachers ministering outside of

the denomination, and the fact that at times denominations may tend to feel they are the one group out of all others that has the correct interpretation of the Scriptures, often rejecting others' viewpoints. Denominations also tend to place *protective* fences around their sheep to prevent them from visiting another pastures (churches). One main issue, however, that does differentiate some denominational from nondenominational organizations concerns the rules and discipline for a minister who has fallen into a sin.

SINS OF THE MINISTRY

In my many years of full-time ministry I have had personal friends who were dear to my wife and me who fell into a temptation or trap of the adversary, yielding to a forbidden act or action, and were exposed, resulting in them stepping down from the ministry for a season. Sadly, some stepped down and never returned to public ministry. Ministry transgressions have included adultery, fornication, unbecoming conduct, incorrect or illegal manipulation of finances, and, as unbelievable as it sounds, in one case the murder of a companion. Some acts are so bizarre that they sound like a Hollywood movie script, such as the case of a pastor whose church was in enormous debt, so he put on a mask and robbed a local bank to get money to pay for his church's building project.

One incident I witnessed firsthand involved a minister who seemed to always be expanding his ministry in every direction. He had purchased a television truck, equipment, a large tent, and was using every tool possible to reach as many people as possible. It was later exposed that much of the equipment in his possession was purchased by phony cashier checks he had printed on a church printing press. At his trial he was described in the paper as a "Christian Robin Hood" who believed his actions were justified because he was using the resources to reach people, even though his methods of purchasing were illegal. He was sent to prison for some time, but today he is out; I think of him often.[1] A more bizarre and sad story was that of a minister who was having an affair and wanted to marry the woman, but he himself was married. He set up his wife on a trip and had her murdered.

Granted, the above are extreme cases and very rare indeed. However, somewhere each week there are ministers, pastors, evangelists, missionaries, or staff ministers whose unrepentant transgressions will catch up with them, exposing them to unplanned embarrassment to themselves, their families, and their ministry. I cannot tell you the thousands of former church members no longer attending a church who were emotionally and spiritually hurt when their spiritual mentor or hero, whom they looked up to, disappointed them and is now viewed by them as a *hypocrite* who did not live what he or she was preaching. This is especially true when the minister is a major media personality with global notoriety. To this day I meet individuals who stopped attending church and have refrained from giving to any ministry because of well-known ministers who confessed to moral sins as far back as the late 1980s. Solomon wrote:

> A brother offended is harder to win than a strong city,
> And contentions are like the bars of a castle.
> —PROVERBS 18:19

Ministers Are Called
Men or Women

People tend to forget that God uses human vessels who have certain flaws and weaknesses. Ministers are selected men (or women) who live in a fleshly house and are subject to the same mental darts, temptations, and trials that all men and women encounter. Two things separate ministers from others: they are the "called" by God and are "anointed" by the Holy Spirit. In Acts we read:

> As they ministered to the Lord and fasted, the Holy Spirit said, "Now separate to Me Barnabas and Saul for the work to which I have called them."
> —Acts 13:2

The Greek word for "called" means, to "call to oneself; to summon or to invite." A person who is *called into the ministry* is someone whom God has ordained from his or her mother's womb to carry the gospel (Jer. 1:5; Gal. 1:15). Any person who is truly *called* must walk in and maintain a high moral and spiritual standard and must, through example, live a life of separation from carnal and worldly pleasures. Paul wrote:

> Come out from among them
> And be separate, says the Lord.
> Do not touch what is unclean,
> And I will receive you.
> —2 Corinthians 6:17

The Greek word for "separate" that Paul used is *aphorizo*, meaning, "to set off by a boundary, to appoint and to limit or divide." This separation to ministry consists of two parts. First, through the call God separates the person to Himself through

His divine choosing. Second, the one who is called must separate himself or herself by living a lifestyle that limits certain types of activity (setting a boundary) that others who are not in ministry may participate in. For example, if a minister seeks the office of a bishop, he must be the husband of one wife. Yet sitting in a local church may be a man who in his past was divorced several times, which would prevent him from entering the office of a bishop (1 Tim. 3:2). A bishop must also be spoken well of in the community, lest he fall into the condemnation of the devil (v. 7). This is why denominations vet those seeking the high office of bishop according to the Bible's guidelines and restrictions.

Just as God placed certain restrictions upon the priests in the Old Testament if they were to minister close to the divine presence, so does He require separation from fleshly desires and carnal thinking more stringently for those whom He calls and chooses.

The second blessing that accompanies the call of God is the anointing of the Holy Spirit. Throughout Scripture the holy oil was used to anoint those separated unto God for His service. The high priests, priests, and kings of the Old Testament were all anointed with oil (Exod. 28:41; 1 Sam. 9:16). David received the oil of anointing as a teenager when the prophet Samuel came to the house of Jesse, David's father. (See 1 Samuel 16.) As the oil was poured upon David, we read:

> Then Samuel took the horn of oil and anointed him in the midst of his brothers; and the Spirit of the LORD came upon David from that day forward.
> —1 SAMUEL 16:13

The sacred oil was the outward sign of God appointing that person for divine service. This oil was to be guarded and not to be poured upon the flesh of a stranger. It was not to be duplicated, so it would not be possible for rebels to attempt to anoint their own priest or king, nor was it to be used to anoint the unsanctified (Exod. 30:31–32). If God guarded the use of the sacred oil compound so carefully, He certainly desires that ministers guard the precious anointing and unction of the Holy Spirit imparted to us for the purpose of effective and powerful ministry (1 John 2:20, 27).

The fact that ministers of the gospel are called, appointed, and anointed requires a higher level of commitment and walk with God than the average person. This responsibility also places the minister in a new light in the *perception* of the people to whom he or she ministers. Whether we like it or not, people within and without the church expect ministers of the gospel to preach the Word and live what they preach. However, what members often forget is that male ministers were *men* before they became *men of God*, and just as Christ was "tempted in all points," ministers are subject to those same temptations. This fact is not a justification for some failure, but it must be understood in light of the human, Adamic nature we all possess. The majority of ministers fall because of one or a combination of PMS—pride, money, or sex.

When Ministers Fail

Having witnessed, observed, and had personal friends who fell into various temptations, I have also witnessed the reaction of Christians within their ministries and those on the outside who become angry and hurt. The following questions are asked:

1. "Why did this happen?"

2. "How did it happen?"

3. "When...who...and what?"

When a minister has fallen and the questions begin flying, I tell the people asking the questions, "Look back over your life as a Christian at your own shortcomings, times when you have missed the mark, and your failures. The enemy attacks the flesh and carnal nature *in each person* in an attempt to draw each person away." The most common disappointment is expressed in the statement, "They preached it but didn't live it."

Before issuing this all-inclusive statement, turning a once-loved minister into a flaming hypocrite, I believe there is a difference between *living a lifestyle* of hidden sin and *falling into temptation's snare* from a single targeted attack. There have been ministers who have been accused of having illicit relations with women in the church who are asked to leave and go to another church, and the accusations follow them from church to church. If these are true, this is an example of *practicing sin*, and eventually this lifestyle will catch up with the transgressor, causing heartache.

However, I have known of cases where the individual lived a solid moral and spiritual life of integrity, but he or she forgot to pray consistently and stay intimate with God, only to find himself or herself in a situation like Joseph in Potiphar's house. In that person's case he or she did not resist and run. The failure was not a sinful lifestyle but a one-time moment of weakness.

For example, when I say King David, people have different images—a teenage giant killer, a man on the run from Saul, and, as almost every knowledgeable Bible student can tell you, a man who fell into adultery and killed the woman's husband. However, have you considered all of the good David did during his entire lifetime, compared to this one major and terrible season of iniquity in his life? Here is how the Bible recalls David's life:

> David did what was right in the eyes of the LORD, and had not turned aside from anything that He commanded him all the days of his life, except in the matter of Uriah the Hittite.
>
> —1 KINGS 15:5

The good of David's seventy years outweighed the sin season, yet his life is marked with one *except*—he did right "*except* in the matter of Bathsheba and Uriah." However, many still connect David's name with adultery more than with his divine destiny. The same occurs today, especially in the case of a moral mess in the life of a minister. Even though there is forgiveness and restoration provided for anyone who truly repents, the one dark mark will always be remembered and, at times, recalled by some, especially by anyone who was hurt in the process.

DEALING WITH AN ERRING MINISTER

My observation over the years is that the process and the public explanation by which a minister's moral failure is handled can either destroy or save the local congregation. There are three important processes to any type of biblical restoration:

1. Repentance of the sin

2. A season of reflection and recovery

3. A restoration back into the call and ministry

Repentance is more than saying you are sorry. It also includes turning from the person or the thing that led to the sin. If a minister was sexually involved with another woman, this would include breaking all ties with her. If the trespass involved misuse of funds, then the minister must remove himself from handling finances. If pride was the downfall, humility and submitting to others in leadership are part of the restoration process.

Take, for example, the failure of Simon Peter. Although it was not adultery or some sexual sin, Peter was dominated with pride, and weakness became the open door for a satanic attack. It was a serious transgression to deny the Lord in front of others! When asked three times outside the trial room if he was a follower of Christ, he *lied* three times by denying Christ. The third time, to prove his point, he also *cursed* and swore. Immediately, however, he felt convicted and went out and "wept bitterly" (Matt. 26:69–75). While Christ's body was in the tomb, Peter had three days to reflect upon his situation. At Christ's resurrection the angel told the women standing near the tomb, "But go, tell His disciples—and Peter—that He is going before you into Galilee; there you will see Him, as He said to you" (Mark 16:7). At that moment there were eleven disciples, for Judas had committed suicide. Notice that the angel emphasized for Peter to also be present at this meeting. To me this indicated that Christ was interested in restoring Peter's ministry and credibility in the presence of the others, who knew of Peter's denial.

Later, when the disciples met Christ on the shores of the Sea of Galilee, Christ asked Peter three times, "Do you love Me more than these?" Peter replied he did love Christ, and Christ instructed Peter: "Feed My lambs"; "Feed My sheep" (John 21:15–19). I believe that by publicly questioning Peter's love for Christ—three times—Christ was releasing Peter from the guilt of the three times he verbally denied Christ. In this example we see repentance by Peter, the season to reflect, and the restoration process of Christ's affirming Peter's love and commitment to Him. *Restoration is a process and not a one-moment event.*

One of the differences between a denomination and a more independent local congregation is that within a denomination there are special boards of elders appointed for the specific purpose of handling the trial process in the event of a proven accusation against a minister. In some instances, in a more independent setting, a minister may be guilty of a charge and simply continue on, and those in disagreement are sometimes simply told to leave and find another church.

As one coming from a denominational background, while growing up there were times when I felt that the systematic methods to deal with erring ministers could be rather cold and heartless, and more of an organized punishment than a repenting-restoration process. For example, a minister found guilty of any moral sin was required to give up his church and sit out of the ministry for one to three years. Some men, after three years, simply never reentered the ministry. They could not even stand and testify, or teach a small group.

When I consider the drunkenness of Noah (Gen. 9:21), the incest of Lot (Gen 19:30–36), the failure of Samson (Judg. 14–16), the adultery of David (2 Sam. 11), and the carnality of Solomon (1 Kings 11:1–8), I often wonder how their sins and failures would be judged by a trial board, and what restrictions would be placed upon them. Certainly there is a process that is painful for erring ministers and members alike. However, the embarrassment, public humiliation, the stress it causes on the family, and the reproach it creates in the church is enough of a *penalty* for the guilty one to bear. Proverbs speaks of adultery and says:

Whoever commits adultery with a woman lacks
    understanding;
He who does so destroys his own soul.
Wounds and dishonor he will get,
And his reproach will not be wiped away.
                        —PROVERBS 6:32–33

The specific negatives that follow this sin are: wounds, dishonor, and reproach. Yet all sins can be forgiven except the sin of blasphemy of the Holy Spirit (Mark 3:29). For any believer falling into sin, there is a threefold process of recovery—confessing the sin is part one, forgiveness of all parties is the second part, and restoration is the third part of the process.

WHAT THE BIBLE TEACHES ABOUT RESTORATION

When Paul addressed the church at Galatia, he rebuked them for starting out in the Spirit and returning to the flesh—or beginning in the Spirit and returning to the Law. In his epistle there is a significant verse that is often quoted when dealing with the restoration process. We read:

Brethren, if a man is overtaken in any trespass, you who are spiritual restore such a one in a spirit of gentleness, considering yourself lest you also be tempted.
                        —GALATIANS 6:1

In this passage the individual was not *practicing* a sinful lifestyle but was "overtaken" in a sin. The meaning of *overtaken* appears here to be a temptation that *gets the better of a person.* Tyndale translated this phrase as, "If a man be fallen by chance into a fault," indicating a sudden temptation or pressure to sin that comes upon a person in a surprising manner—not someone who is deliberately practicing sin.[2]

Consider David and Samson. Samson continually was sneaking around the territory of the Philistines and scoping out the best-looking women. David, on the other hand, arose from bed and saw a woman on the roof—a sudden sight he didn't anticipate seeing. Samson had a major problem with women, but David, on the other hand, was tempted by one woman on one occasion. Be reminded, however, that Samson lost his anointing, and David lost his joy and peace as a result of their disobedience (Judg. 16:20; Ps. 51:1–12). David also lost several of his own sons as a judgment for his transgression. Samson was continually flirting with the devil and, for a season, continued operating in the anointing until the Spirit departed from him. David was flirting with his own passions and found a married woman willing to break covenant for a one-night stand.

Under the new covenant Paul instructed those who are "spiritual" to handle the matters of restoration of the fallen brother. This is very important. If the leadership in a local church setting permits carnal and unspiritual men to initiate the restoration process or to determine the punishment, emotions often overrule Scripture, and opinions are formed from the circumstances and not from biblical guidelines. In several instances carnal elders removed a pastor because of their own ulterior motive to open a door for their own friends to replace the minister. Carnal individuals often seek out the details and feed others, like throwing meat to the sharks. However, spiritual men will discern each situation and act according to the wisdom of God and the Scriptures.

Spiritual men are to "restore such a one." Of course this restoration is contingent upon the sinning person repenting and turning from the thing or person that caused the fall. There are three different Greek words that could be used for "restore." In this instance the word is *katartizo* and means "to mend." Scholars note that in the Greek language the tense is continuous present, suggesting the need for those doing the restoring to have patience and preservation while the process is occurring.[3] When a person breaks a bone, it requires resetting the bone, plus time away from activity as well as patience for the mending process to make the broken bone whole. This is the reason ministers who have specifically sinned are required to sit out for a season. It should not be considered as some form of *punishment*; the reproach is punishment enough. It is a season for repentance, deliverance if necessary, and mending. Many times there must be a healing in the marriage or family, which requires time.

The final part of this verse is important for those who are determining the restoration process of others. Paul warns for the restorers to consider their attitude during the process and remember they are also human and could fall into the same sin trap as the person with whom they are dealing. During my ministry I have observed why Paul gave this warning. On several occasions the very men who were assigned to oversee a trial board for a fellow minister became critical and outspoken of the man's failure. Yet years later they found themselves experiencing the same type of sin and trespass in their own path. Be reminded that Christ said:

> Judge not, that you be not judged. For with what judgment you judge, you will be judged; and with the measure you use, it will be measured back to you. And why do you look at the speck in your brother's eye, but do not consider the plank in your own eye?
>
> —MATTHEW 7:1–3

After speaking of restoring a fallen brother, Paul writes, "Bear one another's burdens..." (Gal. 6:2). In this context Paul is speaking of the heavy burden of temptation that some carry and how we must hold one another up (in prayer and exhortation) to help others overcome their testing. A few verses later Paul reminded the believers that they will always reap what they sow, and sowing to the flesh will always reap corruption (vv. 7–8).

SHOULD A MINISTER RETURN?

Often the question will be asked, "Should a minister return to the same church after his restoration?" This is not an easy question to answer, and I believe each situation may demand a different answer. If a minister started the church or ministry from the beginning, he (or she) normally has more converts and a deeper connection with the people than a minister who was placed in the church by a bishop or a denominational leader. Second, the length of time the minister was in the region or in the local church often has a bearing on this question, as they are more known in the community after years of ministry. Third, the facts surrounding the sin itself may determine the answer. Let's begin with the third statement.

People often say, "All sin is equal." However, this is not true. Yes, sin is sin. But there are sins of *knowledge* and sins of *ignorance*. A sin of knowledge is one in which *much spiritual knowledge is known*. The sin of ignorance is one in which *little spiritual knowledge is known*. There are also sins against people and sins against God. There are sins that people commit involving themselves only, and sins that involve other people. One of the reasons sexual sin is serious is because it involves two people, not just one, and the two are joined as one flesh. The other reason is that sexual sin among married individuals pulls entire families into the crisis, causing more wounds than just to one person. If the sin of the minister involved homosexuality, underage girls, or pedophilia, then it affects the church and entire community, causing the restoration process to extend for many years and often banning the person from any form of ministry, especially with youth. Numerous affairs with women in a church will cause such a breach of trust that it may be impossible for the person to live in the same city or return to the same church after restoration.

Depending upon the situation or the level of sin, if a minister does not return to the same church after restoration, there will always be members who have deep love for the minister, having been converted or touched during the person's ministry, At times these people will leave the church, offended by the church's decision. On the other hand, the same may occur if a restored minister returns to the same church after restoration. Some people may believe the minister who failed has no right to be in the pulpit. Each situation must be determined based upon the minister's repentance and attitude and the congregation's decisions.

Warning to the Judgmental

David warned us not to sit "in the seat of the scornful" (Ps. 1:1). David certainly experienced a terrible failure, and he also endured much persecution, including friends turning against him. Yet David was not overly concerned about his loss of friendships, but he was seriously concerned about the presence of God remaining in his life. He asked God not to take the Holy Spirit from him and to restore the joy of salvation (Ps. 51:11–12). David warned that those who spoke unjustified, critical words would see God turn their own words upon them. (See Psalm 64.) Recently one of my workers told of a woman who was very critical of everyone else in the church, especially when someone's children were in disobedience. It was odd, but several years later, everything she criticized in others she experienced in her own three children— from rebellion, to addiction, to a daughter becoming pregnant out of wedlock!

Being a fourth-generation minister and having personally met tens of thousands of Christians from all major denominations, I have personally witnessed biblically literate believers build a wall of unforgiveness to hold the offense and the offender in a mental castle. The oddest part of this enigma is that some who maintain the tightest strongholds are those who are older in the faith and should know better. In my years of traveling ministry, I was often confused as to why so many elder believers tended to be the most outspoken, opinionated, and the most unforgiving.

The first answer may lie in the upbringing of the individual. I grew up in a traditional full gospel church, which at the time placed emphasis on outward adornment, especially among the women. The female members were not permitted to wear slacks, makeup, or jewelry, nor were they allowed to cut their hair. When a female nonmember attended the church wearing pants, makeup, or jewelry, the judgmental spirit was unleashed like a dam breaking, with tons of uncontrollable water smashing anything in its path. The preaching was often judgmental, which gave freedom to the members to act judgmentally.

I recall a man who owned a business and battled alcoholism who was converted and baptized in the Holy Spirit. When he asked if he could join the church, he was told he could but would not be received into the fellowship until he removed his gold class ring. As a teen I immediately thought, "He is righteous enough for Christ to place his name in the Lamb's Book of Life, but not good enough to join the church? Something is wrong with this picture!" I remember many members who judged people by their outward appearance, which is contrary to how God views us, for it is written: "For the LORD does not see as man sees; for man looks at the outward appearance, but the LORD looks at the heart" (1 Sam. 16:7).

There is a second insight as to why some who have been raised and remained in church struggle with releasing others who are offensive to them. When a woman knelt at Jesus's feet and began to wash His feet with her tears, kissing His feet, some of the "religious folks" felt her style of "worship" was improper. Christ revealed:

> Therefore I say to you, her sins, which are many, are forgiven, for she loved much. But to whom little is forgiven, the same loves little.
> —LUKE 7:47

The most forgiving people in any congregation are those who were previously hard-core sinners. It does seem that the longer people have been converted and remained loyal to a local church, the more they tend to forget what it was like to be forgiven of their own sins, because they have been faithful to the Lord from childhood.

Moses was born and raised in Egypt, speaking the language for forty years. He fled Egypt and lived in a desert for forty years. When God instructed Moses to return to deliver His people, Moses said he was unable to properly speak. Scholars believe he had been out of the presence of the Egyptians so long that he had forgotten the Egyptian tongue, and Aaron, who was living in Egypt, became Moses's mouthpiece. Long-serving Christians can separate themselves from sin and from sinners to the point that they have forgotten *they too* were once sinners.

When you seldom seek God's forgiveness, then the love you should have can be replaced by a judgmental attitude. When an alabaster box of expensive spikenard was broken and poured over Christ's feet as an anointing for His burial, the treasurer of Christ's ministry, Judas, became an outspoken critic of the woman's worship, announcing that the ointment should have been sold and the income placed in the treasury to minister to the poor. Herein are the viewpoints of the two types of church members found in all churches:

1. True worshippers pour themselves out before the feet of the Master.

2. Critics always have their own "better" strategy of doing spiritual things in a carnal way.

When it comes to falling, there are four ways to fall.

1. *Falling forward*—as is falling in the arms of mercy whereby a person willingly confesses his sin and seeks help before any form of exposing occurs.

2. *Falling backward*—when a person is swept off his feet with iniquity and finds himself in a hopeless state lying flat on his back without anyone to reach down and catch him before he falls. These are the wounded ones who take a long time to recover and be restored.

3. *Falling sideways*—whereby a person's sins are exposed.

4. There is one more type of falling down that is the most important and is the greatest preventative medicine—and that is *falling on your knees.*

Living a life of prayer can often prevent you from falling in other directions. It is vitally important to remember that when we think we are standing, we could fall (1 Cor. 10:12). However, it is very difficult to unseat, unbalance, and cause to fall a believer who is praying on bended knees.

Chapter 10

WOUNDED IN THE HOUSE OF MY FRIEND

THE PROPHET ZECHARIAH clearly saw the Messiah's future ministry when he wrote, "In that day a fountain shall be opened for the house of David and for the inhabitants of Jerusalem, for sin and for uncleanness" (Zech. 13:1). The Hebrew word for "fountain" is *maqor* and refers to something dug out, including a water source. The word in ancient times was also used as a euphemism for the flowing monthly cycle of a woman. Zechariah's flowing fountain, however, alludes to the cleansing, flowing power of the *Messiah's blood*, which covers the sinner and initiates redemption to the world, including the inhabitants of Jerusalem.

The further evidence of this indicating a prophetic fulfillment is that when the Messiah returns to earth to rule, His body will bear the marks of His crucifixion. We know this from the Resurrection narrative, when Thomas both saw and felt the scars from the nails in Christ's hands and the spear in Christ's side (John 20:27–28). These same wounds are forever embedded on Christ's body and will be visible when He sets up His kingdom in Jerusalem, as indicated when we read, "And one shall say unto him, What are these wounds in thine hands? Then he shall answer, Those with which I was wounded in the house of my friends" (Zech. 13:6, KJV). He bears the wounds as evidence of the redemptive covenant He provided.

The worst types of wounds a believer can experience are *sacred scars*, which are inflicted by the words and actions of fellow Christians. These internal bruises are caused by cutting words and are most difficult to bear and most confusing to explain. In the past there has been a general attitude in the secular public that confessing Christians should never offend another person and should be willing to take whatever persecution comes their way, without any form of defense or verbal retaliation. Often people will place higher standards upon believers and lesser ones upon themselves. Christians are not permitted to explain their plight or defend their stance, but the enemies of the cross are always willing to use their verbal swords to cut down a believer's reputation, inducing stabbing wounds into the wounded one's spirit to incite a reaction, so they can condemn as unchristian that person's response.

From a political perspective I have seen this *double standard* emerge through the talking heads of certain news networks. When a *conservative* politician confesses to any form of moral failure, the demands from *liberals* to resign are so numerous they sound like a pack of starving dogs smelling red meat from a butcher's truck parked in the back yard. The verbal name-calling begins, and daily news cycles continually demand the *resignation* of this man (or woman) who has failed the public.

Flip the coin to when nonbelieving liberals on the left are exposed taking bribes, caught in adultery, or other forms of iniquity, and suddenly these same dogs stop barking and begin encircling one of their own. Suddenly the cry becomes, "We need to separate the person's value from his or her private life," or "What they do in private is their business." I have also heard, "This is just a political attack." Years ago when a former president had an inappropriate relationship with an intern, the wife went on a morning talk show and accused her husband's failure of being a "vast right-wing conspiracy"![1] When the *Right* fails, it is immoral and unforgivable. But when the Left fails, it is a conspiracy from their enemies.

Morally, culturally, and spiritually America has declined into the pre-stages of the perverted pagan empires of ancient Greece and Rome, as too many in the population are walking around like zombies, pumped up with pot and alcohol, and so doped up that we have entered the *Stoned Age!* Strong Christians understand that the world hated Christ and will also hate us for serving Christ (John 15:18). We have little concern or care when a secular progressive or an extreme liberal feels the need to build his or her ego or résumé by writing against a megachurch or publicly lambasting ministers, attempting to discredit someone they know little about. Our spiritual weaponry in Ephesians 6 is stronger than the darts of a feeble-minded, self-appointed watchdog that barks at the air and chases its own tail for public attention.

There is a vast difference between the cuts of an *enemy* and ones from a *friend.* David experienced a *friend's slash,* and he wrote: "Even my own familiar friend in whom I trusted, who ate my bread, has lifted up his heel against me" (Ps. 41:9). The phrase my "own familiar friend" in Hebrew can read, "The man with whom I was at peace." David was speaking of an inner-circle friend who actually sat at the dinner table, a custom in ancient times where kings invited subjects or intimate friends to eat at their tables. The phrase "lifted up his heel against me" has been interpreted by some scholars as "hath trodden me under his feet."

The idea here is of a horse that turns and kicks the one feeding it.[2] David's integrity and impeccable reputation were in ruins after his affair with Bathsheba and the knowledge that he set her husband up to be slain in battle. (See 2 Samuel 12.) Close friends, including military commanders, turned against David after his adultery and assassination of her husband became public.

The above passage from Psalm 41:9 was a statement related to David's severe trial where he was betrayed by friends, but it also was a future prophecy applied to Judas, who sat at the Last Supper table with Christ, dipping his bread into the cup. Christ predicted Judas's betrayal and told His disciples:

> I do not speak concerning all of you. I know whom I have chosen; but that the Scripture may be fulfilled, "He who eats bread with Me has lifted up his heel against Me." Now I tell you before it comes, that when it does come to pass, you may believe that I am He.
>
> —JOHN 13:18–19

Judas the disciple, the treasurer, and the man from Iscariot—believed to be a town in the tribe of Judah, the same tribal land grant where Christ was from—was called "friend" by Christ at the moment of his betrayal in the garden (Matt. 26:50). It requires a certain level of trust to put anyone over the finances of a major ministry, including Judas overseeing the "bag" (John 12:6, KJV).

Judas told the priests and the soldiers that the one whom he kissed would be the one to arrest. The Greek word for "kiss" used in the betrayal narrative (Matt. 26:48; Mark 14:44; Luke 22:47) is not the normal Greek word for *kiss* used in the New Testament. The Greek word for "kiss" in the above three references is *phileo*, meaning, "to be fond of, to have affection for," and in this reference is used for a kiss that reveals "a mark of tenderness." It was then, and is today, a custom among Middle Eastern men to kiss one another on both cheeks as a greeting and sign of friendship. This custom was practiced in the early church and encouraged by Paul as a greeting among believers (Rom. 16:16; 1 Cor. 16:20; 2 Cor. 13:12). This was a hypocritical act on the part of Judas, as publicly his *mouth* demonstrated friendship but his *heart* was set on betrayal. In this case, actions spoke louder than kisses, and the mouth contradicted the heart. Christ understood that the mouth is actually controlled by the inner feelings of the heart, "or out of the fullness (the overflow, the superabundance) of the heart the mouth speaks" (Matt. 12:34, AMP). Earlier, Satan entered the heart of Judas at the supper after he dipped his bread into the communion cup (John 13:27). The kiss was a lie as the heart was already corrupt. The kiss of friendship was in reality the kiss of death.

Judas is the ultimate example of betrayal from an inner-circle *friend*. Judas is eating, ministering, and fellowshipping with the disciples and the ministry teams. His responsibility to oversee the ministry resources was itself appointed by Christ. Yet there was something in the heart of Judas that transformed this sheep disciple into a Judas goat! Nothing is worse than a sacred scar, a wound from a Christian who was close to your heart but who uses his or her mouth to open a gate of information that cuts to the core of your spirit.

When Kissers Are Cutters

I have shared with friends that I would personally prefer them to speak directly in my face and disagree or express their feelings one on one, rather than have them go behind my back giving their opinions about me or sharing inside ministry decisions. A person outside our circle seldom has any ability to alter a situation, and when adding a second or third person, you are often just pulling others in to agree with your opinion, making you feel right and the other person wrong.

A few times in my life I discovered that a *kisser* was actually a *cutter*, and the face-to-face smiles served to mask a more sinister plot. While you are watching the *kiss*, the hand of the person is reaching around for a solid stab in the back. The pain is not always felt until the information being expressed finds its way back to you, where the wound manifests.

The Oil and the Wine

Luke 10:30–37 reveals the story of an unnamed man departing from Jerusalem on his way to Jericho. During his journey he was attacked by thieves. The robbery left the fellow seriously wounded. A Samaritan (v. 33), a man whose DNA was half Jew and half Gentile, discovered the wounded man and began pouring in the "oil and wine," binding up his wounds. Wine has a certain acid content in it and can kill the bacteria and possible germs the man received while lying on the road bleeding. Oil is soothing and has been proven to be effective on bruises and cuts. Olive oil has numerous healing properties. Thus, there is a twofold application. A person who is emotionally and spiritually wounded must have both the *oil and wine* to fully recover. The wine is derived from crushed grapes, and among the ancients the grape harvest has always represented joy. When you have been verbally abused, betrayed, or struggle in a relationship, the sense of joy is at the bottom of your emotional tank and is difficult to release. Christ should be our example. We read that, when He knew He was headed toward His death: "Who for the joy that was set before Him endured the cross, despising the shame, and has sat down at the right hand of the throne of God" (Heb. 12:2). His joy was not in his *present* circumstances, but it was in knowing the *outcome* of His choice.

Oil is released from crushed olives, and olive oil has always been a representation of the anointing of the Holy Spirit (1 Sam. 16:13). The anointing is the life of God and the energy of the Holy Spirit, which enables a believer to walk in freedom and bring that same freedom to others. When we minister to the hurting, it requires the anointing to break yokes and the joy of the Lord to bring release to the soul.

Notice that both elements—the olives and the grapes— require a *crushing* before releasing the valuable substances of wine and oil. When we are crushed by people or circumstances, we can choose to lie in the ditch as people pass us by, or we can choose to receive ministry, at times from people we least suspect could help us.

In the story of the good Samaritan, both a priest and a Levite passed the wounded man, but they were either unconcerned or too busy with the *work of God* to minister to the poor fellow. The priest is a picture of the Law, and the Levite a picture of the ministry. Neither the Law of Moses nor the temple ministry could bring this man out of his misery. It required the oil and wine from the hands of a Samaritan.

The Samaritans were a *mixed* community who lived in the heart of Israel in a region called Samaria. Devout Jews literally despised the Samaritans. This animosity went back to the time after the Jews returned from Babylonian captivity. Several priests had intermarried non-Jewish women, and Nehemiah demanded they either separate from their wives or exit the ministry (Neh. 13:23–29). One of the grandsons of the high priest had married the daughter of Sanballat, the governor of Samaria. This governor was in charge of a conspiracy to prevent the Jews from rebuilding Jerusalem. This priest left Jerusalem with others and resettled in Samaria. According to Josephus, the Samaritans later constructed a temple on Mount Gerizim in Samaria. This was the same area where the Samaritan woman in John's Gospel questioned Jesus about which mountain was the true place to worship God—in Samaria or in Jerusalem. Thus, these Jews were expelled from Jerusalem, intermarried with Gentile women, and were a mingled people.

It has been suggested that the reason the priest and Levite refused to offer help is because the wounded man himself may have been a Samaritan. If this is correct, it was a form of *religious racism*, as the Samaritans were hated because of who they were and where they worshipped.

Observe that when Jesus, a Jew, journeyed to Samaria, He was not interested in the long-standing Jewish/Samaritan family feud, a religious confrontation, or the argument of a town prostitute who paid no attention to her own sin of sleeping with five men but could debate religion with the best of them. Christ went to Jacob's well, met the woman, and the outcome of this unexpected encounter produced the first evangelist among the Samaritans—an ex-prostitute (John 4:6–29). The method Christ used should inspire us not to argue and debate religion, but to allow the Holy Spirit to minister through His gifts to those who are *rejected* by society, including the many minorities, our own Samaritans, who live in the nation.

Christ's Wounds Bring Healing

Unless a person has studied the *purpose* for Christ's intense suffering, it is difficult to understand why Christ, who was armed with supernatural power, would allow Himself to be humiliated and to suffer abuse and physical pain at the hands of Roman soldiers. When we realize that Christ was an atoning substitute—He took our place—then we realize we are the beneficiaries of the greatest spiritual, emotional, and physical blessings available to mankind. Isaiah the prophet foresaw the suffering Messiah and how He would carry our weaknesses for us. Isaiah wrote:

> But He [the Messiah] was wounded for our transgressions,
> He was bruised for our iniquities;
> The chastisement for our peace was upon Him,
> And by His stripes we are healed.
> —Isaiah 53:5

In this chapter I wish to reveal to you the details of Christ's suffering and how each act of suffering in reality was about you and me. This section was inspired by a close friend, a pastor from India named Samuel Mohanraj, who spoke on the subject, "The Power and Purpose of the Wounds of Jesus." We begin at the trial, with the crown of thorns (Matt. 27).

The Crown of Thorns

> When they had twisted a crown of thorns, they put it on His head, and a reed in His right hand. And they bowed the knee before Him and mocked Him, saying, "Hail, King of the Jews!"
> —Matthew 27:29

When Adam sinned, God cursed the ground to produce thorns (Gen. 3:17–18). Adam would sweat and toil from the ground to produce his bread, or food. When Roman soldiers shoved a crown of thorns on the head of Christ, what was the spiritual significance of this act? To the cruel soldiers, the circular thorns were mocking Christ as the Jewish king. To the Almighty, however, there was a concealed purpose for this action.

The writer to the Hebrews wrote a strange passage in Hebrews 6:8:

> But if it bears thorns and briers, it is rejected and near to being cursed, whose end is to be burned.

Whoever bears the thorns is rejected and is to be burned. Because Christ was accused of blasphemy, after His death on the cross His body should have been removed from the cross, burnt, and His ashes dumped into the valley of Hinnom, a deep gorge on the west side of the city where a continual fire burned, consuming the garbage of Jerusalem. An example of a person's body being burned is found in Joshua 7:10–26, when Achan sinned at Jericho, and he and his family were assembled, stoned, their bodies burned, and their remains placed under rocks in the Judean Wilderness.

At Christ's death a member of the Jewish Sanhedrin, Joseph of Arimathea, begged for Christ's body and then provided his own personal tomb for Christ's burial (Matt. 27:57–58). This action preserved the body of Jesus from being burned or taken by the Roman soldiers to some unmarked grave. Thus, when Christ received the thorns on His head, it was a picture of Him carrying all of the mental anguish His future followers would experience. A rose is beautiful, but all roses grow on stems with thorns. To remove a rose from a bud, the person may be pricked by the thorns. Life has its beauty and its ugliness. At times we are pricked with thorny problems that agitate our minds. Christ became the master of the thorns by wearing a crown of thorns.

THE REED ON THE HEAD

In the pre-Crucifixion narrative, the soldiers struck Christ with a reed:

> When they had twisted a crown of thorns, they put it on His head, and a reed in His right hand.... Then they spat on Him, and took the reed and struck Him on the head.
> —MATTHEW 27:29–30

The Greek word for "reed" is *kalamos*, and it normally alludes to a reed type of plant that grows along the banks of a river. Some suggest the same Greek word can be translated as a "staff." A staff is not thin and light as a reed. A staff is a hard stick. Whether it was a reed from a river or a hard stick, Jesus was repeatedly struck in the head with this reed, which pushed the long thorns deeper into His head. A continual blow to the head will not only cause injury and pain, but it can also affect a person's memory. If these blows to the head had affected the memory of Christ, then He would not have been able to think and speak clearly from the cross in order to fulfill several important Old Testament prophecies.

For example, in Psalm 22 there are numerous predictions that refer to the Messiah's suffering on the cross, including the first verse: "My God, My God, why have You forsaken me?" (Ps. 22:1; Matt. 27:46). I believe the enemy was attempting to dull the memory of Christ before His crucifixion. Had this occurred, Christ would have never made the seven statements from the cross, the thief would never have been converted, and Christ would have never cried out, "It is finished"—which was the final statement the high priest said when the last Passover lamb was offered at the temple! These sayings from the cross were important to fulfill the detailed Old Testament prophecies, types, and shadows of the Messiah. The prophet Isaiah said:

> Can a woman forget her nursing child,
> And not have compassion on the son of her womb?
> Surely they may forget,
> Yet I will not forget you.
> —ISAIAH 49:15

Christ had to retain His memory and not forget that He was the Son of God and His assignment was to redeem mankind. How does this blow to Christ's head relate to us? The fiery darts of the enemy are often sending blow after blow against our minds. The mind is a spiritual battlefield, often flooded with incoming satanic missiles intent on blowing holes of doubt, depression, and discouragement in our minds. The adversary would like for these darts to burn your faith, causing you to doubt God and to forget the promises of your heavenly Father. As the mind becomes weaker, so does your faith. As the enemy deals blow after blow, you become weary in the spirit of your mind.

The loving head of Christ was beaten with a reed because the enemy wanted Christ to forget who He was and what His assignment was about. Christ took the mental blows so that we could rest our own minds in Him and have the mind of Christ in our daily lives (1 Cor. 2:16).

The Spit on His Face

To be spat upon is disgusting and humiliating. Yet Christ endured this, as Matthew recorded:

> Then they spat in His face and beat Him; and others struck Him with the palms of their hands.
>
> —Matthew 26:67

> I gave My back to those who struck Me...
> I did not hide My face from shame and spitting
>
> —Isaiah 50:6

To be spit on is one of the most degrading physical acts. In the Book of Numbers, Miriam, the sister of Moses, had mocked Moses's wife. God allowed leprosy to strike Miriam (Num. 12:10). Moses cried out for her healing, and the Lord answered him saying:

> If her father had but spit in her face, would she not be shamed seven days? Let her be shut out of the camp seven days, and afterward she may be received again.
>
> —Numbers 12:14

Miriam was condemned and expelled from the congregation of Israel for seven days, living isolated with leprosy, just as a daughter would be if her father spit in her face. Afterward God restored her to health.

The act of spitting is also alluded to in Leviticus 15:8. If a person with a running (open) sore spits upon a clean person, the clean person becomes unclean, must bathe, wash his clothes, and is ceremonially unclean for seven days. The Law also taught that if a man's brother died, he should marry his sister-in-law to continue the brother's name by having children. If he refused, the brother's wife was to call the elders together and spit in the man's face for not building up his brother's name (Deut. 25:9).

The act of spitting in the face is an act of condemnation. I am certain some of the Roman guards were familiar with the Jewish law and spat on Christ's face to condemn Him. Condemnation is a powerful weapon in the hands of our adversary. If a child of God sins and does not repent, he will experience condemnation, a sense of guilt for his error. Condemnation is a signal to repent and turn to God. Often, however, a Christian will repent and continue to experience a feeling of guilt and condemnation. The Bible says:

> There is therefore now no condemnation to those who are in Christ Jesus, who do not walk according to the flesh, but according to the Spirit.
> —ROMANS 8:1

As the unclean soldiers spat upon the sinless Lamb of God, it was a picture of Christ taking our shame and condemnation for us. We would no longer be condemned by the unclean works of the flesh or by the condemning voice of the adversary. We would be released from condemnation because Christ carried our condemnation for us.

HIS HAIR REMOVED

Growing up in a traditional Christian church, I often heard some older saints complaining if any minister had facial hair. In my earlier days it was taboo for a preacher to have a mustache, beard, or a goatee. Yet, while viewing photographs of ministers at the turn of the century, I discovered that nearly every minister of every denominational background had a beard, and some beards were very long. Perhaps early ministers read the following passage:

> They shall not make any bald place on their heads, nor shall they shave the edges of their beards nor make any cuttings in their flesh.
> —LEVITICUS 21:5

Among Jewish men in the Old Testament, it was required to grow the corners of their beard. We know the first high priest, Aaron, had a beard (Ps. 133:2), and any Jewish priest who married a non-Jewish woman had his hair plucked (Neh. 13:25). The beard was a symbol of manhood. In ancient times, when an invading army conquered their enemies, the enemy would shave the hair on the head and the beard from those they conquered as a sign of public humiliation.

Long hair was also a sign of a Nazirite vow. No razor was to ever touch the hair of a Nazirite (Num. 6:5). When Delilah shaved Samson's hair, he broke his vow with God and lost his anointing (Judg. 16:19–21). Even a woman's hair was considered a symbol of God's glory covering her (1 Cor. 11:15).

While there is no direct New Testament verse saying that the soldiers plucked the beard of Jesus, there is a prophecy in Isaiah 50 that no doubt speaks of the time Christ was being harassed by the soldiers:

> I gave My back to those who struck Me,
> And My cheeks to those who plucked out the beard;
> I did not hide My face from shame and spitting.
> —ISAIAH 50:6

This amazing prophecy mentions the beating on the back, being slapped on the face, and the spitting. It also alludes to the hair being plucked off the cheeks. No doubt, in keeping with the Law and tradition, Christ grew a beard. The soldiers would have plucked His beard as a public sign of degrading the manhood of Christ and humiliating Him before His peers.

The enemy desires to degrade men. Often male children are void of male attention and affection and grow up seeking attention from a male figure. If this attention becomes distorted, it can lead to attraction to other men in the wrong manner, and eventually a sinful bondage. Husbands and fathers are assigned to be the priest of their home, walking out the spiritual life before their children and being a light in the home.

THE FLOGGING

Who Himself bore our sins in His own body on the tree, that we, having died to sins, might live for righteousness—by whose stripes you were healed.

—1 PETER 2:24

Prior to Christ's crucifixion He was taken to the Roman Praetorium and flogged with a cat-o'-nine-tails. This was a short-handled whip called a *flagrum* with nine long leather straps imbedded with small iron balls and bits of sheep bones at various intervals. The soldiers would strip the victim, tying his hands to a short post protruding from the ground, and stretch the criminal out with his back exposed. Two soldiers often participated in the flogging. As the iron and sheep bone struck the tender skin on the back, it would cut deep contusions into the skin and the subcutaneous tissues. These *stripes* were cut into the person's back, legs, and shoulders. Flogging was often a preliminary act prior to a criminal's crucifixion.

The Romans were permitted to flog a person an unlimited

number of times. The Jews, however, taught that a flogging should be forty times minus one, or thirty-nine times. This is because the fortieth blow could cause death to the victim. Because the Jewish priests were directly involved in the trial, it is suspected that Christ was beaten thirty-nine times.

Because of the blood loss and what medical doctors call *hypovolemic shock*, Christ was unable to carry the crossbar section of the cross to His execution site.

The prophet Isaiah wrote:

> But He was wounded for our transgressions,
> He was bruised for our iniquities;
> The chastisement for our peace was upon Him,
> And by His stripes we are healed.
> —ISAIAH 53:5

Each stripe on Christ's back provided healing! Two beautiful Old Testament pictures of the stripes on Christ are found in the manna that fell in the wilderness and the Jewish Passover bread. When God rained manna in the wilderness—angel's food—it was called the "bread from heaven" (Exod. 16:4). It was white in color and similar to a coriander seed (v. 31). A coriander seed is a small seed that has very tiny furrows across the outer shell. Christ was the manna come down from heaven, and this manna seems to have the imagery of the stripes of a coriander seed! The Jewish Passover bread, called *matzo*, is baked with small holes and has long rows that are similar to furrows on both the front and back sides.

Jesus was the "bread from heaven" (John 6:31–38). Just as the manna was crushed in order to produce food to eat, so the body of Christ was beaten to bring us life! Some have suggested that Christ was beaten thirty-nine times, and there are thirty-nine major diseases from which all other diseases originate. One fact is clear. The stripes on the back of the Savior are for our healing! Jesus carried our sicknesses so that we could be healed. This is clear from Matthew 8:17:

> That it might be fulfilled which was spoken by Isaiah the prophet, saying: "He Himself took our infirmities and bore our sicknesses."

I like the Amplified translation, which makes it clear:

> And thus He fulfilled what was spoken by the prophet Isaiah, He Himself took [in order to carry away] our weaknesses and infirmities and bore away our diseases.

In the ancient temple on the Day of Atonement the high priest would lay his hands upon the scapegoat, praying a prayer to transfer the sins of Israel onto the goat, who later was led into the wilderness and pushed from a cliff. Why would Christ be pictured as the goat on the Day of Atonement? I once had a goat farmer tell me that a goat could literally take on the sicknesses of other animals. He once had sheep with abscesses, and he placed the goat among the sheep to take on the abscesses of the sheep. In a few weeks the goat had so many abscesses that it died! One older minister said, "Jesus was made sin with our sins and sick with our sicknesses." This is why, in the Garden of Gethsemane, His sweat became as great drops of blood (Luke 22:44). Christ was experiencing the weight of the world's sins and the weight of sickness in His own body.

Paul revealed that Christ the sinless lamb was made sin for us:

For He made Him who knew no sin to be sin for us, that
we might become the righteousness of God in Him.

—2 Corinthians 5:21

The New International Version reads this way:

God made him who had no sin to be sin for us, so that in
him we might become the righteousness of God.

The flogging brought physical, spiritual, and emotional
healing to us through the stripes of Christ.

The Rejection Factor

Isaiah said the suffering Messiah would be "despised and rejected
of men." When reading the Scriptures, we overlook the power
of this prophecy. After Christ's birth, numerous infants were
slaughtered because Herod was attempting to slay the infant
Jewish king (Matt. 2). Perhaps some blamed the infant child's
birth on the others' deaths. As a child He lived in Nazareth, a
small town with this reputation: "Nazareth! Can anything good
come from there?" (John 1:46). His own hometown folks tried
to throw Him off a cliff in Nazareth after He preached His first
sermon (Luke 4). When He ministered, there were times He had
no place to sleep (Matt. 8:20). The multitude of common people
received Him, but the religious hierarchy sought to trap Him
and eventually set out to kill Him. At His trial His disciples
fled (except John and Peter), and eventually Peter buckled under
peer pressure, going on a cussing spree to prove he didn't know
Christ. The multitude He healed failed to even be present to
defend Him, and Jerusalem was in an uproar to see this tall sun-
tanned Nazarene punished by crucifixion. It sounds like Christ
knew rejection from humanity from the moment a jealous king

sent soldiers to kill Him until the time that Roman soldiers hung Him between heaven and earth on a hill called Golgotha!

Rejection takes on various forms and different levels. Children especially gain their self-esteem from their parents, siblings, and friends. Growing up, when someone had braces they were called "metal mouth," and children with glasses were teased for having "four eyes." Overweight boys were labeled "fat Albert," and the girls were just told they were *fat*. Skinny and often small-statured children were bullied, and a youth attempting to be a Christian was fair game to any unbeliever. These words stung and became seed in the spirit that grew into a tree of rejection.

Christ was called a devil and accused of working miracles by demonic power. Combine that treatment with the religious opposition from numerous Jewish and political groups, and it is obvious He endured much verbal opposition. Christ carried our rejection so we could be released from its binding grip.

Two Cents Worth of Love

If the lack of love or abuse you endured growing up has affected your own relationship with others as an adult, this illustration may help you release the past and press into the future.

One of our family's friends is a distinguished woman eighty-four years of age. She is also connected with our youth outreach ministry. Her heart was always turned toward prisoners, addicts, and those without Christ. She related to me that her mother was a beautiful yet verbally and physically abusive woman. She felt she could never please her mother and was always being reminded of every time she failed and didn't meet the standard. She grew up, married, and as she matured into a wife, she had difficulty and sought out a counselor.

After hearing of her mother's lack of love and how it affected her, the counselor said, "Would you accept all of the money I have today to give you?"

Knowing it must be an illustration, she replied, "Yes."

He pulled out his wallet and there was no money in it. He then pulled out a checkbook from his desk and showed her the account was empty. After searching, he found two cents in his pocket—just two copper pennies—and he handed them to her. He asked, "Are you mad at me?"

She said, "Of course not!"

He said, "Why?"

She replied, "Because that was all of the money you had, and you gave me all you could give me."

It was there he made the point. "Your mother gave you all of the love that she knew how to give. She only had two cents worth and no more. Don't be mad when that was all she had and all she knew how to give!" The illustration brought freedom to her.

The rejection you have felt from childhood was perhaps ignorantly fed by family members who themselves never knew love or were raised in a home where love, attention, and affection were not a part of their own childhood. When my father and his father were children, the men in the house believed you were a *sissy* or *weak* if you cried at all. In that day fathers seldom hugged their children, as that was what moms did and not dads. Fathers in those days used switches from trees, leather belts, and their hands to discipline (actually it was a *whipping*) their children; they could at times be angry with their words in the process, calling the offender all sorts of names, laced with profanity. If your own parents grew up in this type of culture, they themselves may not know how to express love in actions or words other than cooking, cleaning the house, doing laundry, or in a father's case, working to provide. I know of older women in their seventies who were raised in a strict, not affectionate home, and if you go to hug them, their hands are at their sides because they are uncomfortable with any expression of affection.

It may be that two cents of love was all of the love your mother, father, or siblings were able to give you. If that amount was all they knew and all they gave, do not be angry, but make up your mind that you will love your life in Christ and give His love to others. Your fulfillment in life is not where you have been, but it is where you are going!

Chapter 11

THE RISE OF THE BROTHERHOOD OF BLOOD

IT IS SAID that "blood is thicker than water," which I believe is evident especially among nations birthed through tribal ancestors. The power of blood loyalty is evident in the Arab culture. It is forbidden to discredit or disgrace the father, leader, or older men in the Arab culture. Years ago when an American president made a decision to "take out" a vicious Arab dictator, he was restrained by a powerful Arab king in the Gulf, who said, "This man is a dictator and is evil, but in our culture you cannot disgrace him before the Arab people!"[1] This type of loyalty is called *Arab honor* and has resulted, even in America, in what is called *honor killings*, when a father would actually kill his own daughters for disgracing the family.

One of the strongest *brotherhoods* that controlled the gambling, drugs, and prostitution in America for many years was the Mafia. When a man was positioned into the ranks of the mob, an induction ceremony pronounced blessing upon him for maintaining the mob's secrets, and curses were pronounced upon the inductee if he ever revealed the secrets to outside sources. One of those curses was that he would die of terminal throat cancer if he ever spoke out forbidden information. In the 1970s one man who infiltrated the mob was turning over criminal evidence against the mob in a federal court, but he was near death—dying of terminal throat cancer.[2]

There is a reason so many inner-city youth join gangs. In many poverty areas there is a shortage of biological fathers to protect and raise sons in a strong, loving environment. When a young man is "tapped" for gang membership, to prove his loyalty he must first fight with the entire gang, or steal something of value, or even kill someone, or a combination of all three. After fulfilling the "mission," he will be inducted into the gang and be given specific gang colors, in return receiving the backing of all gang members for protection. This is one example of a brotherhood of blood in which each member swears an oath to die for the other. Many times young men join gangs for the protection and promise to be defended from outside enemies.

One of the oldest forms of a brotherhood is with a group of men called *Masons*, who use special code words, secret handshakes, and temple rituals to bring a fellow Mason into their lodge. These secrets are to be kept under a vow. Many men who join this group do so for what they say are "business reasons." The fact is that this old secret order that has been in America for centuries is another example of a brotherhood.

These forms of brotherhoods are natural, secular, and even carnal in nature. Yet the most important brotherhood in the world is the covenant Christ cut through His death and resurrection, forming a spiritual family for all who enter the new covenant. As believers we call each other "brother" and "sister," terms used in a biological family for a physical brother and sister. The origin of the word meant someone birthed from the same womb.

When a mother is carrying her child within her womb, the infant is in water. At birth both blood and water manifest when the infant exits the birth canal. Throughout Scripture blood and water were double weapons that defeated the powers of darkness. The blood of the lamb on the doorpost and the closing of the waters of the Red Sea crushed the armies of Pharaoh and brought the kingdom of Egypt to its knees. In the temple in Jerusalem the water of the laver and the blood of the sacrifice combined in bringing ceremonial and spiritual cleansing to the worshipper. At Christ's death both blood and water poured from His side with the thrust of the centurion's spear, sealing the redemption process for eternity. We are saved by the blood of the Lamb and sealed through the water of baptism! In a natural family blood puts you in the family of your flesh, and water baptism introduces you to the family of the Spirit, the family of God. Receiving the blood of Christ and the water of baptism indicates you are in covenant with God through Christ.

The earliest God-ordained covenant is the covenant of marriage. When a woman is a virgin and consummates the marriage with her groom on their honeymoon, she sheds a small amount of blood, which indicates the proof of her virginity. This physical manifestation was designed by God as a covenantal act, since a woman can only enter this type of a *blood* covenant with one man. The proof of virginity was so significant under Mosaic law that if there was a question of the bride's virginity, the sheets must be shown to the elders to prove it (Deut. 22:13–19). The original intent was for one man and one woman to enter a covenant of marriage for life. Divorce only became a provision because of the hardness of men's hearts (Matt. 19:8). The Old Testament opens with a marriage in Eden (Gen. 2), and the Old Testament ends with a marriage of God to Israel (Mal. 2). The ministry and first miracle of Christ began with a marriage (John 2), and the

Book of Revelation climaxes in heaven with a marriage supper (Rev. 19).

We must each enter this covenant *one on one* with Christ, as no one can enter it for us or on our behalf. After righteousness through Christ is imputed to us, we maintain our covenantal agreement publicly before God and men through daily Communion. The act of drinking from the cup, which contains the fruit of the vine, and eating the bread is a picture of the blood and body of Christ, reminding us of His redemptive sacrifice.

The main point is that we, the body of Christ, are linked together as one family of God through the blood of Christ and the water of baptism. Notice how blood is significant in all forms of covenants. When God created Adam, he breathed the breath of life and man became a living being. God imparted within Adam the substance of blood, since the "life of the flesh is in the blood" (Lev. 17:11). The Hebrew people were to circumcise the flesh of the foreskin of each male child on the eighth day of his birth as a sign of his covenant with God (Gen. 17:11). Upon consummating the marriage, the bride seals her covenant with her husband with blood evidence. We enter the family of God through the blood of Christ, which washes us of our sins.

> And He has made from one blood every nation of men to dwell on all the face of the earth, and has determined their preappointed times and the boundaries of their dwellings, so that they should seek the Lord, in the hope that they might grope for Him and find Him, though He is not far from each one of us; for in Him we live and move and have our being, as also some of your own poets have said, "For we are also His offspring." Therefore, since we are the offspring of God, we ought not to think that the Divine Nature is like gold or silver or stone, something shaped

by art and man's devising. Truly, these times of ignorance God overlooked, but now commands all men everywhere to repent.

—ACTS 17:26–30

THE FAMILY OF GOD

While many men join gangs, secret orders, and tribal units for the purpose of brotherhood, men both young and old in the body of Christ must understand the *brotherhood of blood* forged through the covenant of Christ's redemptive blood. If we are such a brotherhood, why are we not acting like it?

One of my staff members once worked closely with men in the US military. After watching the close-knit brotherhood of the military, with its respect for authority and emphasis on honor and integrity, she commented that, "Men who play together become competitive, but men who fight together become brothers." The spirit of competition is found in the Christian community in every town and city in America. I recall years ago seeing a Christian satellite network battle a major Christian network and was amazed how one was mistreating the other. In retrospect, each was only concerned about its own "turf" and saw the other as an intruder. Churches compete for members, attendees, visitors, and especially over finances, as there is only so much money available for ministry. Many congregations internalize their battles and even make the church across town their "competitive enemy." This is because they are not warring in the same battlefield. Soldiers in the same war need one another and need the strength of their brothers to sustain them when bullets are whizzing and shrapnel is flying. Our enemy is not an opposing denomination, a pastor in the next county, or members who have left our church; our enemy is Satan, and our goal should be the same—to break the powers of darkness over men and women through the gospel!

Adoption into the same family

There are four primary elements that make us the family of God (Eph. 3:15). The first fact is that we have been adopted into the same family! In Romans 8:15 we have received the Spirit of adoption. In Galatians 4:5 we have been redeemed to receive the adoption as sons. In Ephesians 1:5 Paul revealed that we have been predestined to adoption as spiritual children through Jesus Christ. An adopted child maintains all of the civil and legal rights of a natural-born child, which means that each adopted believer is on equal standing with one another, and one is not more superior to the next. We have a common adoption.

The same Father

The second truth is that as adopted children we all have the same Father in heaven. Paul wrote that we all have "one God and Father of all, who is above all, and through all, and in you all" (Eph. 4:6). The Almighty is the Father of this family with children in heaven (those who have passed and are in the heavenly paradise) and those on earth (alive and anticipating the return of Christ).

The same city

These adopted children of the Most High have an inheritance in the same city, called the New Jerusalem or the heavenly Mount Zion. The writer to the Hebrews wrote:

> But you have come to Mount Zion and to the city of the living God, the heavenly Jerusalem, to an innumerable company of angels, to the general assembly and church

of the firstborn who are registered in heaven, to God the Judge of all, to the spirits of just men made perfect.

—HEBREWS 12:22–23

If you plan on living in the heavenly city and inheriting the New Jerusalem, then I have a great suggestion that you learn to get along with your brothers and sister in Christ in this life! When a family moves all of its children into one house, perhaps for economic reasons, the main message is, "Get along with each other." How can we expect to have unity when we get to heaven when we can't practice unity on earth?

The same heavenly registry

The fourth important aspect of this brotherhood is that those in covenant adoption have their names recorded in the heavenly registry, called the "Lamb's Book of Life" (Phil. 4:3; Rev. 3:5; 13:8; 21:27). In the time of the Jewish temples, when a priest stood to be inducted into the priesthood, certain physical defects could disqualify him. If he was examined and received, he was given a white robe, and his name was inscribed in the priestly records at the temple.[3]

We have entered this spiritual family through one source: the blood of Christ that has redeemed us. Let me refer back to the words "brothers and sisters." According to Greek scholar Rick Renner, the word *brother* was used in the time of the great Greek general Alexander the Great, when he would stand on the platform a warrior who had performed great military feats in battle and would say, "Alexander the Great is proud to be the brother of this soldier!"[4] Thus, *brother* was used among the Greeks to identify a person who warred together with another in the same warfare.

I regret that in the church we have made enemies of our

fellow believers. I have actually heard wonderful, godly Christian ministers called "enemies of the cross" and "heretics" by self-appointed and self-anointed delusional watchdogs of Christianity. These watchdogs often declare that they alone teach "solo truth" and are the only ones on the planet anointed, appointed, and chosen to carry the gospel to the world. When James and John rebuked others for ministering to the sick who were not from their group, Christ rebuked them, revealing that He had "other sheep" that were not of the disciples' flock (John 10:16). When James and John cried out for Christ to burn up Samaria and kill the Samaritans by calling fire out of heaven, Christ rebuked these "sons of thunder" (Mark 3:17) and said, "You do not know what manner of spirit you are of" (Luke 9:55). Even Peter took on the attitude that Gentiles were wrong in not receiving circumcision, and Paul had to withstand him to his face for his lack of understanding of the Gentiles' relationship in the new covenant and his apparent hypocrisy of ministering to the Gentiles then later avoiding them altogether (Gal. 2:11)!

How can any believer who treats other believers as enemies expect to spend eternity with them and sit beside them at the marriage supper of the Lamb? Jesus did not teach: "They will know you are My disciples by the amount of income you bring in a year…how many radio and television stations your voice is heard on…or the number of buildings required to run the ministry." He said, "You will know them by their love for one another and by the fruit produced by their actions." (See Matthew 6:16; John 13:35.)

A Lesson From
the World

It was Christ who said in Luke 16:8, "For the sons of this world are more shrewd in their generation than the sons of light." In my early ministry the revivals would continue for three to eleven weeks in length, often resulting in as many as fifty to six hundred people being converted to Christ in every meeting. My greatest joy was the new converts, and my greatest frustration was the follow-up. Most of the rural churches had never had so many baby lambs (new converts) in their congregation at one time, and the general attitude was, "Well, if they are really saved, they will go to church and live right." The older saints, who were comfortable in their "green pastures" were often in a *flight* mode instead of a *fight* mode—that is, they were unwilling to fight for life and growth of these younger believers. Instead they left them on their own to the elements and the wild beasts, being unwilling to take the time to teach, instruct, and pray for them to mature into strong believers.

In the secular world, once you enter into a gang, a secret order, or are born into a particular culture, the family members surround you, guaranteeing protection and that your needs are theirs and their blessings are yours. This is where the world is beating up the church. We spend all of our energy on programs that should attract them like flies to honey, or creating opportunities for them to visit our facilities. Let's be real. We cannot compete with the money of Hollywood, the fleshly excitement generated by rock concerts, and the weekends at the bar by simply patting them on the back, joining hands, and singing, "Hallelujah." New buildings get old, old programs get boring,

boring services are filled with empty pews, and empty pews prove the sinners are missing!

There are two things all human beings need that the church is supposed to provide: the first is love, and the other is relationships. Without either, your local church pews will eventually be in a lumberyard a generation from now. The Christian brotherhood should not be based upon a denominational emphasis, with your emphasis on church membership, but upon a holy nation emphasis (1 Pet. 2:9), with relationship outweighing membership. The world is used to the club days where everything centered on the club. They left the club and don't need to join another club, or they would remain where they were.

At OCI Gathering Place, in my hometown of Cleveland, Tennessee, we have hundreds who attend services each Tuesday night. Among the group are many new converts, former drug addicts, ex-alcoholics, and some who are coming out of an alternative lifestyle. We often hear visitors comment that there is such an atmosphere of love and acceptance in services and that the people are very community and relationship oriented. We have anointed worship and great preaching, and in years I have never seen a "boring" or "dry" service. However, it not just the services, but it is also the friendships, fellowship, and relationships being built that have attracted the unsaved to the Gathering Place. Love is expressed in words, and love will manifest in actions.

Chapter 12

THE POWER OF LIFE AND DEATH
IS IN YOUR MOUTH

ECENT RESEARCH HAS proven that the words of Solomon can be taken literally: "Death and life are in the power of the tongue, and those who love it will eat its fruit" (Prov. 18:21). This research covers three areas: a rice study, a water study, and a plant study.

Several years ago I received information from research done by Gary Townsend, who began a study on how words can affect specific substances, in this case rice. The research began on April 1, 2008. Gary cooked a batch of organic basmati rice in one pot. The rice was then distributed equally into two clear glass jars of the same type. Gary ensured details were the same in the preparation and sealing process. The jars sat in the same place side by side from April 1 to June 22 (about eighty-one days). After the time concluded, in one sealed jar the rice remained white, and in the second jar the rice had turned moldy. The only difference between the jars was the words written on paper that had been attached to the jars. The rice that remained white had the words "I love you," and the moldy rice jar had the words, "You are bad rice—I hope you die," with the date April 1, 2008.[1]

During our main conference in Hixon, Tennessee, I showed the pictures of the jars and gave the details of the study. Some in the congregation found it difficult to believe that words written on paper could affect rice, which has no ears to hear or eyes to see. A group of youth from a church in Oklahoma decided to conduct their own study by speaking to similar jars of rice— positive loving words to one jar, and negative words to the other jar. After an extended time they were amazed to see that the jar receiving the loving words had white rice, and the other was beginning to turn color.

Dr. David Van Koevering, a close friend and a man trained and experienced in the power of sound and words from a scientific perspective, sent me his research from a second experiment using water.[2] When sharing this information, Dr. Van Koevering reminded me that all humans came from the earth, and we consist of a physical body that returns to dust.[3] Our bodies consist of a large volume of water. For example, the brain is 75 percent water, and the body's weight is 60 percent water. Blood is 92 percent water, and human bones consist of 22 percent water.[4]

To demonstrate how words have power to change the molecular structure of water, Dr. Masaru Emoto, a Japanese researcher, did a documentary on the effects of words on water. His theory was that thoughts and feelings affect all forms of physical reality, whether written thoughts, spoken words, or music, and water molecules are altered accordingly. Dr. Emoto used a high-powered microscope, a cold room, and high-speed photography to document his research and photograph water molecules. He noted that some water will not crystallize from polluted springs. The research discovered that frozen water crystals actually change with certain words and music.

In the study a cup of water drawn from a spring was placed

in a room where people were assigned to make either negative or positive statements. A small amount of water was poured from the cup into a petri dish and frozen at -25 degrees Centigrade for three hours. The frozen water was removed and examined under a powerful microscope, magnifying the crystals two hundred to five hundred times in a cold room that was -5 degrees Centigrade, to prevent the crystals from melting. What Dr. Emoto saw was stunning. Crystals that had heard the words, "Thank you very much," "Love and appreciation," and other positive statements had formed the most beautiful crystals, similar to the shapes of snowflakes. On the other hand, the water that heard the words "Idiot," "Ugly," "You disgust me," and "I am going to kill you" had no crystal shape whatsoever; they had lost all form.[5]

An Israeli chemistry student named Tomer Rabiavi attended a lecture in which the research of Dr. Emoto was being presented. The student was inspired to conduct his own research, this time using white beans placed on a bed of cotton in three different petri dishes. On the first he placed tap water without uttering or thinking anything. On the second he pronounced curses, and on the third he spoke psalms from the Book of Psalms. In two weeks the beans with normal tap water began barely sprouting on the dish. The beans that were cursed were still on the cotton bed and had not sprouted or grown. The beans that had psalms and blessings spoken were not only sprouting but also were already several inches high![6]

Rice, water, plants, and humans all have one thing in common: they are all from one Creator—God—and they all consist of atoms and molecules that hold all things together, invisible to the human eye. Atoms join together to form molecules, which in turn form the objects around you. Atoms are composed of three particles: protons, electrons, and neutrons. Protons have a positive electrical charge and neutrons a negative electrical charge. These are the invisible forces that are holding all life forms together.

In 1938 German physicists Otto Hahn and Fritz Strassman split the atom, generating fission—released energy. This process eventually unleashed the world's most dangerous discovery, the invention of the nuclear bomb. Certain biblical miracles, such as turning water to wine, require some type of a molecular change in the atom particles. Even walking on water defies gravity. When Christ spoke to a sickness, His words contained such power and authority that He could reverse a sickness, initiate a cure, or introduce a creative miracle. Jesus revealed that His words are "spirit, and they are life" (John 6:63).

Many years ago a noted evangelist was ministering in Kentucky, and my friend was driving him to his speaking appointment. A discussion ensued of the power of words. The evangelist said, "I don't discuss this publicly, but my wife has many plants on the back porch, and when they seem to be struggling in their growth or the edges turning brown, she asks me to go pray in the room, as she has noticed that if I do my devotions in that room, her plants seem to remain green and even grow faster." Before a person considers this impossible, new research has proven that plants can actually respond to the type of sound being emitted in the same room.

A study cited by the British magazine *Nature* described the work of an internationally known Indian researcher and a pioneer in studying plant life, Sir Jagdish Chandra Bose, who had studied how plant life responds to all forms of stimuli. His discovery indicated that plants can express sensations in ways that can be measured by science. Bose's discoveries were reported in *Nature*, and in the Russian newspaper *Pravda* the headlines announced, "Plants Speak. Yes, They Shout!"[7]

Dr. T. S. Singh was head of the Department of Botany in India. He heard rumors that music was having an impact on plants, causing them to grow faster and appear healthier. Dr. Singh set up a scientific experiment in a lab in which he played three types of instruments at specific distances from the plants and observed the plants produced more seed and grew at a greater rate. After hearing of his discoveries, tests were conducted on rice fields using loudspeakers for sixty minutes a day. The average field yielded an increase of 25 percent to 60 percent more rice.[8]

Before you think that plants or trees are not subject to words being spoken, consider the fact that Christ and His disciples passed a fig tree, bearing leaves, and Christ cursed the tree:

> Now in the morning, as He returned to the city, He was hungry. And seeing a fig tree by the road, He came to it and found nothing on it but leaves, and said to it, "Let no fruit grow on you ever again." And immediately the fig tree withered away.
>
> —MATTHEW 21:18–19

If rice, water, plants, and trees can have words of blessing spoken that affect them, how much more can either positive or negative words have an impact on human beings, who possess a soul and spirit?

How Words Affect the Blood

The Bible indicates that the life of the flesh is in the blood (Lev. 17:11). It has been known for many years that all diseases in the human body can be discovered in the blood. Each year I have a major checkup to determine the condition of my body and my health. The first test conducted is to draw blood, and the doctor then views a three-page printout analyzing my blood and indicating the conditions occurring in my body based upon specific and identifiable levels and counts in the blood.

Since the life of the flesh is in the blood, how do anger, stress, and other negative emotions affect the blood itself? First, we know that anger causes an immediate rise in the heart rate and a rise in blood pressure. It has been proven that stress, coming from both physical and especially emotional sources, affects the hormone cortisol, which is produced by the adrenal glands. The purpose of cortisol in small amounts is to assist as an anti-inflammatory, and it also helps to speed up tissue repair. However, a rise in the cortisol level is bad, because raised cortisol levels from stress can cause immune cells to disappear from the blood, causing your immune system to plummet. According to one doctor who deals with cancer, a sudden surge of strong anger can actually shut down the immune system up to six hours. According to researchers, if a person is living under continual stress and producing unhealthy levels of certain hormones being released in the blood, a serious illness is usually preceded by a major cause of stress.[9]

The apostle Paul gave an interesting statement to the church at Corinth concerning the physical condition of many members in the church. This church was a strong and growing congregation. However, division was occurring because of envying, strife, and divisions among the believers (1 Cor. 3:3). Paul addressed the issue of the division and then gave instructions concerning receiving the Lord's Supper, or the Eucharist. These believers were not taking seriously the significance and the sacredness of the holy meal. Paul gave the church this warning:

> Therefore whoever eats this bread or drinks this cup of the Lord in an unworthy manner will be guilty of the body and blood of the Lord. But let a man examine himself, and so let him eat of the bread and drink of the cup. For he who eats and drinks in an unworthy manner eats and drinks judgment to himself, not discerning the Lord's body. For this reason many are weak and sick among you, and many sleep. For if we would judge ourselves, we would not be judged.
> —1 CORINTHIANS 11:27–31

In the redemptive covenant the physical body of Christ was bruised and beaten for our redemption from sin. Christ endured a beating, called a *scourging*, with a Roman whip, an event predicted by the prophet Isaiah when he wrote:

> But He was wounded for our transgressions,
> He was bruised for our iniquities;
> The chastisement for our peace was upon Him,
> And by His stripes we are healed.
> —ISAIAH 53:5

This scourging provided physical healing for believers who are in covenant with Christ. The crucifixion of Christ was for the healing of the spirit and soul of a person who receives Christ's atoning work, accepting Him as Lord and Savior—the forgiver of our sins. During Communion the bread represents the body of Christ, and the fruit of the wine represents the precious blood of Christ. How can a person receive unworthily and thus bring damnation upon himself?

The prime example is Judas, one of Christ's twelve disciples.

At the Last Supper, where Christ was breaking the bread and drinking from the cup, thereby introducing the new covenant, Judas himself dipped his bread in the cup and partook of the supper. The problem with Judas's action was that Satan had entered his heart to betray Christ (John 13:27). Because his heart was corrupted, he was not participating in a *sacred rite* but merely performing *a religious routine*. Notice that shortly after receiving the money, Judas ended his own life (Matt. 27:5; Acts 1:16–19).

If the majority of all sickness and disease is traceable through our blood, then your healing is linked to your willingness to forgive others and keep your *bloodline* strong.

The Word Wrapped in Flesh

Christ Himself was born of a virgin, without the necessity of a man's natural seed. Christ was the Word of God wrapped in flesh (John 1:1–14). Christ was made sin for us, and "He has borne our griefs and carried our sorrows" (Isa. 53:4). Matthew 8:17 quotes Isaiah's prophecy, and it is correctly translated to read: "That it might be fulfilled which was spoken by Esaias the prophet, saying, Himself took our infirmities, and bare our sicknesses" (KJV). Christ's blood helps the secret power of forgiveness, as He was not tainted with the original sin of Adam, because He was born of a virgin!

Christ was beaten, mocked, and crucified, and every nerve, muscle, and cell in His body were screaming out in pain. Yet He found the strength to cry out to God: "Father, forgive them; for they know not what they do" (Luke 23:34, KJV). Christ was to become the only High Priest over our faith, and He could not die with unforgiveness and maintain the heavenly priesthood.

By not forgiving, He would have forfeited His authority to forgive others. Christ's sacrifice would have been made void without His forgiving all who had wronged Him. Christ would not die with unforgiveness, as unforgiveness is a sin! Herein is a very important point. On my part it requires the blood of Christ being applied by faith to my spirit in order to receive forgiveness and eternal life. However, once I have received His forgiveness, I must then forgive others; otherwise I will void the blessing, favor, and forgiveness of God in my own life. Look at this verse:

> For if you forgive men their trespasses, your heavenly Father will also forgive you. But if you do not forgive men their trespasses, neither will your Father forgive your trespasses.
> —MATTHEW 6:14–15

Blood is spiritually significant. When Cain slew his brother Abel, God said that the voice of Abel's blood was crying from the ground (Gen. 4:10). During the Tribulation the blood of countless martyrs will cry out to God for vengeance (Rev. 6:10). We can also recall that at the death of Stephen, Stephen forgave those murdering him. Saul of Tarsus was overseeing the execution, and this same Saul would later be converted on the road to Damascus, illustrating that no sinner or religious zealot is too hard to reach.

While the stones of his critics were gnashing upon the head of Stephen, he had an open vision and saw Christ "standing at the right hand of God" (Acts 7:55). Seeing Christ "standing" may seem insignificant; however, Christ is presently the High Priest in the heavenly temple. Using Old Testament patterns, on the Day of Atonement the high priest was not permitted to stand as long as he was performing any function related to the ritual of using the atoning blood to expedite sins. Only when the entire day had concluded, and forgiveness was sealed in the eyes of God, could the high priest sit down and rest from his activity. When the high priest stood, it was to perform a specific ritual related to mediating between God and himself, the priests, or the Israelites.

From an ancient temple perspective, when the priests sat, the work was complete, and when they stood, it was to receive a blood offering for sin, trespass, thanksgiving, or a feast offering from the people. Stephen was asking the heavenly High Priest, Jesus Christ, to make intercession and forgive his accusers and his murderers. Christ was standing not only to receive the spirit of Stephen at his death but also to forgive the transgressors of their terrible acts.

Without his knowledge, Saul of Tarsus was ordained by the Lord from his mother's womb to preach the gospel to the Gentiles. As he watched Stephen's death, at that moment he was unconverted and was a legalistic Pharisee who believed he was doing God's service by eradicating these cult members of the Nazarene. Stephen's blood was not spilled in vain, as the voice of forgiveness was just another key to unlocking a door to the conversion of Saul of Tarsus.

Many years ago in India a precious native missionary and his wife were attempting to reach a village, when a group of Hindu radicals rose up in opposition and slew the husband in order to prevent a Christian church from being built. The woman, instead of retaliating or quitting, purchased the ground that was mixed with her husband's blood and began to make clay bricks, and she built a small building for a Christian church.

It is often easy to tell others, "I love you," when they already love you. It is a total "God thing" for you to love your enemies and pray for those who persecute and despitefully use you (Matt. 5:11, 44). Our ministry supports numerous missionaries, many who travel to remote third world nations, including some countries that are still Communist controlled. At times underground pastors are arrested, beaten, and at times tortured for their faith. Some missionaries have returned and told me the most amazing stories, that the guards in charge of the beating were eventually converted to Christ because of the steadfast faith and the ability of a persecuted believer to tell their enemy, "I love your soul, and I am praying for you."

Christ shed His blood to redeem us from the prison house of the enemy (Eph. 1:7; Col. 1:20) and to begin a new family called "The Family" (Eph. 3:15). This family is a brotherhood and a sisterhood of blood! We are all made one, by the blood of Christ (1 John 1:7).

Chapter 13

SEASONS IN THE LIFE OF A SHEEP

SOLOMON WROTE: "To everything there is a season, a time for every purpose under heaven" (Eccles. 3:1). Sheep and goats are found grazing in the same fields. While this book focuses upon the characteristics of Judas goats and their conflicts among the flock, it must be pointed out that good sheep also have their seasons in life and their own internal and external difficulties that must be dealt with. The New Testament was written in a cultural setting where agriculture was the primary business, and thousands of shepherds cared for flocks along the Judean hills and the Galilean communities. When Christ spoke to the multitudes in an outdoor setting about sheep, goats, and shepherds, His words were an illustrated message, as often listeners could see these objects in view. In the Gospels, Christ is considered the Good Shepherd, and believers are the sheep in His pasture (John 10:11–16).

In November of 2007, during a Holy Land tour, our group toured a site in Bethlehem known as "Shepherd's Fields," a large, rugged piece of real estate perched on the edge of the city, owned by the YMCA. Our tour guide, an Arab Christian named Bassam, was raised in the area and was very familiar with raising and caring for sheep. He gave a lengthy and extremely interesting lecture on the various seasons in the life of sheep, comparing them with Christian life experiences. I believe you will find the information interesting, practical, and at times amazingly parallel to the Christian experience.

FIVE INTERESTING FACTS ABOUT SHEEP

The Hebrew word for *Bethlehem* means, the "house of bread." The region was known for its barley and wheat fields. (See the Book of Ruth.) Bethlehem is noted as the hometown of King David, himself a shepherd, and is better recognized as the birthplace of Christ. The lambs that were selected for the morning and evening sacrifice at the temple in Jerusalem (located about six miles away) were all born and raised in Bethlehem. Bethlehem is filled with caves, and archeologists have discovered caves that were used to secure the sheep at night. In biblical times each shepherd watched between thirty and fifty sheep. At night the sheep were in danger unless the shepherd placed his sheep in a cave.

We learned that sheep do not take care of themselves, but they must have a leader to follow and to care for them. In the time of the prophets and of Christ the people of Israel were often compared to sheep without a shepherd—a nation of people who were spiritually wandering aimlessly without clear direction and whose lives lacked spiritually from a lack of spiritual leadership, or shepherds. All sheep of any age require a shepherd to protect, direct, and instruct them, especially when considering the dangers sheep encounter in the Judean wilderness setting.

Such dangers include ledges with steep drops into dangerous gorges, poisonous serpents concealed under stones and hiding in bushes, loose rocks near cliffs that could dislodge (sending the sheep rolling down a mountain to its death), certain plants that, if eaten, could cause sickness, and of course the occasional wild, sheep-eating beasts. These common dangers required the watchful eye of a strong shepherd trained to watch and protect his flock from any internal and external dangers.

Sheep also require much attention on a daily basis—*not just once a week*. In North America the traditional Sabbath, which is Sunday, is viewed as a one- or two-hour worship and preaching setting, when all the sheep and baby lambs come together in the same pasture to hear a message from their shepherd. However, there are six other days in a week in which the *God flock* will encounter wolves, serpents, wild beasts, and unique dangers, requiring the attention of leadership to help them avoid the traps being set by the enemy. A believer must do more than participate in the comfort of a two-hour worship service and then leave the security of the church and spend six days working among wolves who have no interest in the Christian faith or spirituality. We all need the fellowship and relationships we make in the house of God and must have quality time feeding off the life that is in the Word. The shepherd's care is not just for 120 minutes on Sunday; his watchful eyes and listening ears must be aware of the distant roar of a lion or approaching storm.

We were informed that sheep often find themselves in danger because they are "dumb animals" and can be easily spooked, especially when they sense danger. Remember, it is their nature to *run from* trouble instead of *facing* trouble, and they depend upon the voice and hands of the shepherd for their protection. It is human nature for spooked sheep to leave a church if the church as a whole is entangled in some form of trouble or negative publicity. If a local congregation is in financial debt and needs large offerings, some sheep-members will attempt to find an exit strategy, as they feel self-induced pressure that may require them to give additional offerings for payments owed to the bank. When a pastor morally falls and the shepherd is removed, the sheep in the flock do not always accept the new "voice" they hear from a new shepherd and often depart from the flock, as it is their inbred nature not to engage in a troublesome or confusing situation, but to flee in the opposite direction. Serious conflict seldom unites believers in a church; it usually divides the group. The wisdom of a shepherd must always be superior to that of the sheep.

Sheep are also known to enjoy sticking their necks out into another man's pasture! They are always poking around in a field near their own, claimed by another shepherd, as at times the grass seems greener and more appealing. In my hometown of Cleveland, Tennessee, there is an inside joke among the many pastors as to which church their former members are now attending. Our county, which has a population of about 90,000 people, has more than 340 churches, and there is as much variety in local churches as on a food buffet that has different types of food. It is common in our city for some sheep to cycle through three or four different churches in a period of five years, looking for the perfect shepherd-sheep match. It is the nature of sheep to wander from one field to the other if the boundaries are not set. As one man once said, "The greener grass in the other field may be because of a leak in a septic tank, and not just due to the planting of green grass from the farmer or shepherd." Keeping your flock well watered and fed is a key to keeping them loyal to your pasture.

Sheep can be easily distracted by their surroundings, which includes insects, flies, bad weather, and dangerous storms. These distractions can cause sheep to react in a manner that brings danger to their own lives. Many years ago in New Zealand a sudden storm struck over a large field where thousands of sheep were grazing. Suddenly air-to-ground lightning began to strike, causing the sheep to panic. A large number began running, causing a panic in the entire group, until a massive number were running full speed across the field. The momentum of their panic led them to a cliff, causing the sheep to fall to their death below, costing the lives of thousands of sheep. It was mass panic.

Flies and insects are little agitations that harass the sheep. It is the "little foxes that spoil the vines" (Song of Sol. 2:15), and often the small distractions that hinder the most—not the massive challenges. For example, some church members waste energy arguing over the style of music, the level of the sound system, and the fact they can't park close to the front doors, thus permitting opinions to become the insects that distract their focus.

THE SEASONS IN THE LIFE OF A SHEEP

When Christ used the analogy of His followers being sheep, He was certainly aware of the seasons in the life of a natural sheep and how these same seasons are parallel to the seasons found in the lives of believers.

The rut season

First there is the season of what some term *the rut*. In Bethlehem, trails that the sheep (and goats) have made are visible on the sides of the mountains, as sheep are creatures of habit and do not enjoy any form of change from their routine. They will graze in an area, walking back and forth over the same area until ruts are formed, altering the terrain. How true this is for a local church. Year after year people park in the exact same parking spot, sit in the same pew, shake hands with the same people, and sing the same songs; when their routine is broken, they become carnal and upset if you lead them away from the rut they have formed. Just as ruts impact the condition of the pasture in a field, ruts and routines in a local church will impact the atmosphere and attitude of the worshippers.

The lambs, or the younger generation in the church, are a generation that is into the Internet, cell phones, iPods, iPads, texting, movies, YouTube, and Facebook; they are always on the move with a slight attention deficit. They bore easily and are not thrilled in the least with a normal routine. Remember this: *a rut is simply a grave with both ends open!* There will be an exodus of baby lambs if the church service is viewed as a rut and routine. The remedy for breaking out of ruts is for the shepherd (pastor) to initiate new programs and outreaches to keep the people motivated and reaching out beyond the four walls of their own church. Any ministry activity is linked to vision, and it is the shepherd's vision that causes people to follow the ministry. Without a vision, the people perish (Prov. 29:18, KJV).

The season of head butting

The second season that occurs at some point will be when sheep become agitated during the summer heat and begin to bump heads against other sheep. If this process continues without intervention, the sheep can actually create small scabs on their heads that over time become infected. These types of scabs can spread throughout the flock, causing more discomfort among the sheep. This "head-butting" factor is often observed among the older, more seasoned believers in a church, especially among board members and elders in leadership, each having their own opinion as to how to operate the church ministries. The butting heads represent the carnal thoughts in the mind of believers that are expressed through negative words and enacted with negative actions of the leadership. When verbal disagreements cause a clash of opinions, the head shepherd must do what a Middle Eastern shepherd would do—the shepherd takes the sheep with the scab and plunges its head in a tank of water to wash the head and prevent infection. Before meetings get out of hand, stop the board meeting, and demand prayer to be offered to renew the minds of the "head butters," and read scriptures from passages in Proverbs that will renew the minds of those present.

During the hot summers in Israel, numerous types of flies are buzzing throughout the area, and this can bring great danger to the sheep. Unlike humans, natural sheep have no hands and fingers to scratch where it itches! Flies can lay their eggs in the nose membranes or on the head of a sheep. When the eggs begin hatching, the itching causes the sheep to rub its head against a rock or a tree, thereby causing a serious infection. In areas such as Jericho, the summer fly season brings literally thousands of flies into the region. I have been on tours when the bus doors opened and flies would begin to pour in. We would see twenty to fifty at one time around the windows and buzzing around the tourists.

Sheep Christians can open the doors to the flies, which are serious agitations in life that affect their walk with God and their friendships with others. The remedy for the fly eggs laid on the head or the membranes of the sheep is a mixture of olive or linseed oil with some sulfur and a black tar-like substance that the shepherd rubs on the head of the sheep. This kills the eggs, preventing them from hatching. This is perhaps why in the great Twenty-Third Psalm David identified the Lord as his shepherd, writing, "You anoint my head with oil" (v. 5). The oil identifies the Holy Spirit's presence, which pours over the mind of a believer, providing power to break mental yokes and bondages. Having ministered tens of thousands of times, I have discovered that there is no better source of spiritual and mental renewal than the precious anointing of the Holy Spirit.

During the summer in Israel the sheep enjoy the high hills and the bright warm sun. However, the shepherd must bring them into the valley where the clear water is flowing. The mountains of Judea are very dangerous and steep; the paths between the two can be slippery and steep. Therefore, to move from the high hills to the low place, there is a walk through the "valley of the shadow of death" (Ps. 23:4). The journey brings a danger of serpents and wild beasts, and the journey from the mountain to the valley is risky. In our faith tradition the mountains are the spiritual high places where we bask in the light of God's glory, the warmth of His presence, and we tower above the problems and dangers below. However, we cannot always abide on the mountain, but must at times journey into a valley, passing through many dangers. However, Christ is with us through the "valley of the shadow of death" and has promised to never leave us or forsake us (Heb. 13:5). Light is clear on a mountain, but water is found in the valleys.

Even the change in the seasons of the year can bring changes in the attitudes of the sheep. During the fall months (a picture of the harvest) the male rams will begin to battle for dominance. Their clash with other male rams is designed to get the attention of the female ewes, as mating season begins in the fall months. Perhaps you have seen this activity on television documentaries, where two rams stand head to head, clashing and battling with their horns, or *locking horns* in an attempt for one to dominate over the other. These battles can actually become dangerous, and a ram can be wounded.

This natural action is reflected in the spiritual realm, as at times the leadership in a local congregation (especially in times of growth or harvest) will begin to butt heads with one another and *clash* over how to handle situations and who should be in charge. A growing church may threaten the control of some dominant members who feel they are losing their grip as elders or board members. There is always one ram in every church who dominates important business conversations and decisions, and if these rams do not get their way, they flex their strength by controlling others, including conversations or events, which can lead to unnecessary conflicts. These types of clashes were seen in the early church when the leadership was struggling over the teaching of circumcision among the Gentiles, arguments about how the Gentiles fit into the new covenant, and discussions about what laws a Gentile should obey. In Acts 15 it was the apostle James who soothed the issue by quoting a prophetic passage and giving basic instructions that were received by the other apostles (vv. 13–22). A good shepherd will stand between the two opposing groups, taking control of the clash before wounds are inflicted.

The cure for such harsh head butting is to place heavy amounts of oil on the horns of the rams, which become slippery, acting like grease when the rams lock horns. The use of oil in the Bible is often a picture of the anointing of the Holy Spirit. A special mixture of olive oil was used to anoint the kings, priests, and, at times, the prophets in ancient Israel (Lev. 8:12; 1 Sam. 16:13). It is the responsibility of the shepherd to provide the oil and to initiate the "rubdown" on the horns of the opposing factions. I have known of ministers who would call the two divisive sides together, instructing them to pray for one another face-to-face. It is difficult to be angry with someone you are praying for—and impossible to curse and bless a person in the same prayer!

The "cast-down" season

One of the most interesting seasons in the life of a sheep is found in Psalm 42:11, where David wrote:

> Why are you cast down, O my soul?
> And why are you disquieted within me?
> Hope in God;
> For I shall yet praise Him,
> The help of my countenance and my God.

The psalmist spoke of being "cast down." In English we think this term means, "depressed, sad, or in a bad mood." However, to a shepherd overseeing a flock, the ancient term speaks of another season that occurs in the life of the sheep. At times a sheep can lose its balance and roll over on its back, unable to get back up on its own. As internal gases begin to build and expand within its intestinal area, eventually the circulation can be cut off in its legs. This is what is meant by being "cast down." To us humans, it means to fall down and be unable to get back up.

David spoke of this season in his own life when his soul was cast down and he became so discouraged that he felt he was unable to pick himself back up. David battled giants, Philistine armies, and even his own father-in-law King Saul for numerous years. A combination of battles occurring all at once will eventually wear a person out emotionally, leaving that person feeling cast down and isolated. Two reasons for a sheep becoming cast down can be when that sheep becomes too *fat*, causing a lazy feeling to overcome it, or when too much wool covers the sheep's body, meaning he needs to be sheared.

When a sheep is cast down, it is the responsibility of a good shepherd to pick up the sheep and begin to rub its legs to bring proper circulation to the animal and to help it get moving again. We often hear of a person becoming *depressed*, a word that literally means, "to lie down flat." A mentally depressed person is someone who feels so low that he cannot lift himself up without help from an outside source. When Moses raised his hands with the rod of God, Israel prevailed in battle. When his hands slipped down, Israel began struggling. Two men, Aaron and Hur, stood on either side, propping up the arms of Moses to ensure a victorious outcome for the Hebrew nation (Exod. 17:10–12). At times you must have others who will stand with you and undergird you through prayer, counseling, and support until the battle is won!

Seasons of storms

Finally, there are seasons of the storms that come in life. There are natural and spiritual storms that can impact our families. Natural storms such as hurricanes, tornadoes, blizzards, and earthquakes can destroy property, homes, cars, and other possessions. Recently in our hometown an F-4 tornado struck the city, leveling homes to their concrete foundations in certain areas. Men can *predict* a storm but not *control* a storm. Spiritual storms include the death of a loved one, marital conflict or divorce, a child addicted to narcotics, or a sickness that strikes you or a loved one unexpectedly. It is not always a hard rain that spooks sheep. The sound of thunder and the sight of lightning— a combination of what they *see* and *hear*—can strike restlessness in their hearts. Just so, our faith can be shaken by what we see and hear.

The famed Sea of Galilee is known for its unexpected storms. Some rare storms are caused by an underwater earthquake that happens occasionally, as the sea sits in the middle of the Syrian-African rift that was formed by ancient volcanoes, and the sea is subject to small tremors or, at times, large earthquakes. The most common storm is created by winds blowing across the high mountains, forming a whirling effect in the bowl-like waters of the lake. Jesus and the disciples were caught in both types of storms, called *a tempest* in the New Testament (Matt. 8:24). During these storms a rider in a boat can *see* the waves and *hear* and feel the violent winds. In March of 1992 a storm struck the area, sending ten foot waves from the lake, which crashed down on buildings on the shore. One moment the sea can be as flat as a glass mirror with no ripples, and moments later the waves may be churning and a storm has begun.

When you live in central Tennessee and the Weather Channel tells you a blizzard in the west is headed to the east, you have just enough time to rush to the store for bread and milk, fill up the car with gas, and get winter clothes out in case icy tree branches snap and break power lines. However, there will be times when the sky is clear, and just five minutes later hail begins to fall and a tornado is outside your window—and there is no time to run and hide. Life brings bad news with a sudden phone call, an unexpected crisis, and sudden spiritual storms. Every believer needs a shepherd—a pastor, a minister, or a special person—to be there when the thunder is so close it deafens your ears and the lightning is blinding your eyes. The trust that sheep place in the shepherd, hearing his voice and sensing his presence, comforts them in time of storms.

THE NEED FOR GOOD SHEPHERDS

The one person who has the greatest responsibility and ability to deal with goats and comfort the sheep in these seasons are good shepherds. Just as with a cattle rancher, every shepherd places a physical mark on his sheep to identify them as his own. True believers have a seal called *the seal of the Holy Spirit of promise,* enabling the Holy Spirit to mark us as one of God's children (Eph. 4:30). For a Spirit-filled believer, the manifestation of the prayer language of the Spirit is a physical manifestation that marks a believer as set apart in covenant with Christ and baptized in the Holy Spirit (Acts 2:4; 10:46; 19:6). Thus, the Spirit places a *mark of spiritual identification* upon those who belong to the Good Shepherd.

A true shepherd is assigned to guard and protect his flock and must also *set a watch* over his pasture to ensure that wild beasts or thieves are not permitted to enter and kill or steal the precious sheep (John 10:10). Christ spoke of being the Shepherd and being willing to lay down His life for His sheep (v. 15). In ancient Israel, at night the shepherd would place his sheep in a cave and surround the entrance with thick branches, piles of stones, or other objects to prevent the sheep from escaping into the dangerous night. The shepherd would then lay his entire body at the small main entrance; thus if a sheep tried to exit the security of the cave, it must pass over the body of the shepherd. This demonstrates how the Good Shepherd is willing to lay down His life for the sheep.

As indicated previously, the pasture is the local church. Each good pastor will protect his members and attendees from hirelings who would take advantage of them (John 10:12–13) and from wolves in sheep clothing ("false prophets," Matt. 7:15). It is also noted that when sheep produce baby lambs, the mother and the lamb must be provided a higher quality of food than what is normally provided. Our churches must not become "adult nurseries," pampering and petting an overfed group of settled sheep who often overrate their importance and underrate their spiritual performance. Our churches must provide effective ministry for the children and teens in the congregation. The fact is, if we don't relate to this generation, then the lambs will grow up and eventually be lost to the wild beasts surrounding the field.

The water provided for sheep must be clean and trouble-free flowing water. Before I listened to the lecture from our Israeli tour guide, I was unaware that fast-moving and *restless water* will cause a sheep to become hesitant to drink and nervous. During the summer it is best to find a cooler area with palm trees, or an oasis where a fresh underground stream is flowing in the desert.

DISCIPLINING THE SHEEP

One important act of a shepherd that few believers enjoy discussing is that a shepherd must at times discipline the sheep. Spiritual sheep have a tendency of staying away for no good reason or of simply wandering too far away from the flock, personally endangering themselves. Some animals have a natural built-in GPS system and can find their way home with little effort. However, sheep can act independently, stray, and get lost, with no idea how to get back to the group. This is often the condition of a backslider—a person who has served Christ but was pulled back into sin and the world. Such an individual is considered a "lost sheep" and must be reached by the shepherd, who, according to Christ, should leave the ninety-nine sheep and go find the one lost sheep to recover him and bring him back into the flock.

In my opinion, the average church has failed in its responsibility to rescue the *one lost sheep*. One man told me, "Before I received Christ, I couldn't keep the Christians away who told me they loved me and were praying for me. I received Christ but months later fell into sin. It was at that point—when I became a prodigal sheep—that I couldn't figure out what had happened to all those loving and caring Christians. Before my conversion I felt like I was a deer and they were the hunters, and once they got me as a victory trophy, they went on to find their next trophy."

I have known of people who were absent from church for weeks and never received a phone call to inquire about their condition. It's more comfortable to camp out, roasting marshmallows and telling Bible stories around the bonfire with the ninety-nine well-fed sheep than to leave the comfort zone and search through a dangerous wilderness to find the lone sheep. A good shepherd will discipline (and warn) a wandering sheep before it gets to the place where it separates completely from the flock.

Every ancient shepherd carried three important items: a slingshot, a rod, and the staff. The slingshot was used to sling stones at dangerous or unwanted animals, and the ancient shepherds were masters of this simple weapon, as observed in the story of

David slaying Goliath. (See 1 Samuel 17.) The staff is the long stick, usually about five to six feet tall, that a shepherd leans upon and uses to balance himself on the hillsides. It is also used to walk on the round ledges of the hills and can be used to tap on stones to determine if they are stationary or loose. In the Judean wilderness there are vipers and small poisonous serpents who pose a danger to any sheep. These snakes often conceal themselves in trees or small bushes along the regular path walked by the flock. A shepherd will lead the flock, shaking the bushes with his rod to see if he shakes any snakes from the bush, killing them before they bite one of his sheep.

The rod is a smaller piece of wood about the size of a baseball bat, narrow at one end and thicker at the other, that serves as an extension of the shepherd's arm. Some shepherds made a hole and tied the rod to their belts, and others placed nails at the end in case it was needed to strike a dangerous beast. The shepherd gives the sheep freedom to roam on a field. However, if a sheep changes direction, making its own plan, the shepherd will hit the ground several times as a warning. If the sheep persists in rebellion, the shepherd will use the rod (or a staff) and tap the sheep on the head to get its attention. If the shepherd sees a sheep straying too far from the flock, he will sling the rod in its direction, startling the animal and causing it to run back to the security of the flock. Thus the rod was used for correction and at times as a weapon against dangerous beasts.

The rod is also used at times to tap the back legs of a sheep to get its attention. At night, before the sheep enter a cave or a secure area, the shepherd allows the sheep to pass under the rod and be counted (Ezek. 20:37).

Here is what every pastor, staff member, or future pastor needs to know.

- Sheep must have a *head*, a leader or a shepherd to follow.

- They must be *led*, as they are created to follow and are not natural-born leaders.

- They must be *fed* in the green pastures of God's promises and the water of the Holy Spirit.

- They must be *read*, meaning a minister must understand their thinking process and think ahead of them to prevent dangers from arising.

- They must have a *bed*, or a place to lie down in rest.

While there is always concern for the Judas goat, the majority of challenges for any church or pastor lies in understanding these seasons of the sheep. The shepherd must know how to successfully deal with each season and assist the sheep in coming through these life cycles with peace, confidence, and joy.

The sheep can never rest unless three things occur:

1. The sheep must be well fed.

2. They must have plenty of fresh water and have been refreshed.

3. They must feel secure.

If the ministry is not in order and fails to provide any one of these three ministry provisions, the sheep will become nervous and unable to enjoy rest.

My grandfather and father were both pastors. Each had many good sheep in their flock. But there were at times a manifestation of a goat who would butt his or her way into self-appointed authority on boards, attempting to control everything from the type of people who were "welcomed," to the way the income was spent, and to the style of music. At times a few goats would run off some good sheep as the sheep became weary with the words and attitudes of the goat members. It is better to deal with and at times "expel from the flock" one angry goat than to watch sheep and their little lambs walk out the door and never return. When strife arises in the church, it requires a time of repentance and confession to restore order to the congregation.

Chapter 14

RELIEF GIVEN BY CONFESSION

WHEN AN INDIVIDUAL is guilty of a crime and faces his or her moment in the court before the judge and jury, defense lawyers are appointed to prove the guilty person is innocent, often despite evidence to the contrary. The alleged guilty person often refuses to *confess* to any crime, and through lack of *evidence* the lawyers lay out a case to persuade the twelve jurors that their client is not guilty by creating *reasonable doubt*. Thus, in a human court, an apparent criminal often refuses to confess guilt in hopes of being cleared of the charges.

The court of heaven is quite different, although the heavenly temple is set up similarly to a court scene. In the Apocalypse and various additional scriptures, we see where God, the judge of all men, is seated upon His throne. Before the throne are twenty-four elders, representing twelve men from the old covenant and twelve men from the new covenant—perhaps the sons of Jacob, who will judge men and women who lived in their time and under the Law of Moses, and the twelve apostles who will assist at the judgment of those who lived under the new covenant. (See Revelation 4–5.)

Christ is called our "Advocate" (1 John 2:1) and serves as the

High Priest who makes intercession for us (Heb. 7:25), weighing the evidence for or against a person as it is presented by the prosecuting lawyer, Satan, who is called the "accuser of our brethren" (Rev. 12:10). The witnesses in the heavenly court are the hosts of angels surrounding the throne of the great judge.

The heavenly court is the only court in the universe where, when a person stands and confesses, "I am guilty. I am a sinner; I have sinned, and done wrong," that person can then ask for a pardon after admitting his or her *guilt* and *receive* a pardon instead of a penalty! This act of admitting our guilt and asking for pardon is a process initiated by something the Bible calls "confession." Confession is not just important, but it is also necessary when a person is seeking to enter a redemptive covenant. We read in Romans 10:8–10:

> But what does it say? "The word is near you, in your mouth and in your heart" (that is, the word of faith which we preach): that if you confess with your mouth the Lord Jesus and believe in your heart that God has raised Him from the dead, you will be saved. For with the heart one believes unto righteousness, and with the mouth confession is made unto salvation.

John also noted the power of confession when he wrote:

> If we confess our sins, He is faithful and just to forgive us our sins and to cleanse us from all unrighteousness. If we say that we have not sinned, we make Him a liar, and His word is not in us.
> —1 John 1:9–10

John said we should "confess our sins," and Paul said we should "confess Jesus Christ." In context, Paul's statement in

Romans refers to a person who is *initially converted* to Christ and enters the new covenant through receiving Christ's blood and atoning work on the cross. In Paul's day the Greeks and Romans had numerous false gods, and their followers offered incense and financial and animal offerings in temples. They would swear oaths and promises using the names of their gods. Christianity was based upon the death and resurrection of Christ and His position of being the Son of God and offering Himself as the final sacrifice. Entering this covenant requires a repentance of sins, which refers to a turning from a sinful life and confessing that Christ is your Savior and Lord. After entering the covenant, it is still possible for a believer to sin, and thus the words of John become significant.

John is writing to the church to remind them that if they walk in the light, they have fellowship with Christ, and His blood cleanses them from all sin (1 John 1:7). He follows up with, "If we confess our sins..." (v. 9), Christ will cleanse us, and "If anyone sins, we have an Advocate with the Father" (1 John 2:1). Thus the significance of confession is found in our initial repentance and in our progressive walk with God.

There is a very dangerous doctrine that is spreading in the body of Christ, teaching that once we have initially repented, all of our future sins are also automatically forgiven, and there is never a need to repent again. Those teaching this doctrine apparently have not fully understood either man's sin nature, the warnings given to believers who have sinned, or the many places the Lord instructs believers who should sin to repent.

The best example of believers being commanded to repent is when Christ is addressing the seven churches in the Book of Revelation. Among these seven, only two—Smyrna and Philadelphia—were commended by Christ and given special blessings for their faithfulness (Rev. 2:8–11; 3:7–11). The other five churches (Ephesus, Pergamos, Thyatira, Sardis, and Laodicea) were all encountering serious spiritual issues—some with false teachers, false doctrine, sin in the leadership, or being lukewarm. In four specific references Christ commanded the churches or individuals to repent of their sins or their sinful actions, or else He would introduce some form of judgment against them (Rev. 2:5, 21, 22; 3:3, 19). Without repentance Christ would "remove your lampstand from its place" (v. 5) or "cast her [specifically a false female teacher]…into great tribulation" (v. 22), or He would "spit you out of my mouth" (Rev. 3:16, NIV). If the sins of those within the church were automatically covered, there would be no command to repent.

John addressed the issue of a believer who may have sinned when he wrote:

> My little children, these things I write to you, so that you may not sin. But if anybody sins, we have an Advocate with the Father, Jesus Christ the righteous.
>
> —1 JOHN 2:1

John taught that believers should not sin—that is, they should not practice a lifestyle of sinning. He did say that "if we sin," which indicates it is possible to sin; we as believers are not *exempt* from temptation and could "fall into a sin" by being overcome with mental pressure and darts from the enemy. Thus, *if* we sin we have "an Advocate" in heaven, who is Christ. Why is there a necessity of having an advocate in heaven after becoming a repentant believer if an advocate is never needed again and confession is never required again? An advocate is a mediator in a court case, and Christ is in heaven, dealing with Satan, who is the accuser of the brethren (Rev. 12:10).

The Meaning of
Confess and Confession

There are two Greek words meaning "confess" in the New Testament:

1. The first is *homologeo*, from two words: *homou*, meaning, "same," and *lego*, meaning, "to speak; to speak the same thing." This is the word used when Scripture instructs us to confess our sins (1 John 1:9).

2. The second word is *exomologeo*, a word used when Paul alluded that all men will "confess that Jesus Christ is Lord" (Phil. 2:11), and when James admonished us to, "Confess your sins to each other...so that you may be healed" (James 5:16). This word means, "to verbally acknowledge something," whereas the first word, *homologeo*, means to publicly (verbally) come into agreement with someone, and also carries the connotation to "ascent, accord and agree with, declare and admit."[1]

When we confess our sins, there are several dynamics occurring at once. First, our confession that we are a sinner is admittance to the fact that we acknowledge our guilt, enabling us to be released from the condemnation of sin. This confession is two-fold: admission of our condition and asking for God's intervention. As we confess our sins, or the fact we are a sinner, we are also admitting we need a Savior, who is Christ the Lord. By confessing our sin and need for a Savior, we then are in agreement with the promises of the Word of God; thus we and God are saying the same thing and agreeing on the same thing.

It was James who gave us the most significant understanding of the need for believers to confess their faults to one another in order to be healed. In fact, healing is actually contingent upon a believer's having a proper relationship with other believers. James wrote:

> Is anyone among you sick? Let him call for the elders of the church, and let them pray over him, anointing him with oil in the name of the Lord. And the prayer of faith will save the sick, and the Lord will raise him up. And if he has committed sins, he will be forgiven. Confess your trespasses to one another, and pray for one another, that you may be healed.
>
> —JAMES 5:14–16

This passage is not addressed to sinners but to believers. The emphasis here is upon confessing your "faults" (KJV). The Greek word for "faults" in this passage means when a person has "side-slipped or deviated into some type of error." Among members in a local church, this would include any form of contention, discord, strife, bitterness, unforgiveness, or jealousy, as these works of the flesh often creep their way into the attitudes of carnal individuals. When approaching God for any type of healing, James gives a process of calling on the elders, anointing with oil, praying in the name of the Lord, and exercising faith. However, your own spiritual blessings and, in this case, your own healing are contingent upon your spirit being free from any type of bad feelings or negative attitudes toward others.

There is a relief that comes by confession. Many years ago I was ministering in North Carolina, at the church of Pastor Billy

Franklin, the father of my close friend Jentezen Franklin. Pastor Franklin was one of the greatest men of God a person could ever meet, and the Franklin family (and relatives) were and are some of the most godly, praying people you could ever know. I knew nothing about the church, its past or present, as when I ministered I wanted to have a clear mind, enabling the Holy Spirit to speak to me without any advance knowledge or personal preconceived ideas.

I recall a large attendance one Sunday morning and Sunday night. However, the services were very tight, and I sensed a strange undercurrent in the congregation. On Monday night as I stood to minister, the Holy Spirit came upon me, and I said, "I am not going to preach tonight. We are going to have a public confession service, as there is terrible strife in this church, and the Holy Spirit will not move and bless until some of you get the junk out of your hearts."

Then I said, "Here is the microphone, and I am going to sit down. You need to confess your faults to each other and repent to one another and to God." About eighty people sat and stared at me, and I looked at them. Finally a young girl stood, whose father was a minister caught in a moral failure and had lost his ministry. She began crying and telling the church how they had gossiped about her dad and not tried to restore him.

People broke down weeping. Suddenly people stood up and began to repent of bad feelings and attitudes. Before the service concluded, people were hugging, weeping, and rejoicing. The next night the attendance doubled, and without making any effort, people came to publicly repent and confess their bad attitudes, which had hindered them and others. The following night the place was packed, and revival began breaking out. The entire atmosphere of the church changed as a result of confession.

When two people are at odds, only *pride* prevents them from correcting the error of the contention. Usually each person feels justified in his or her emotions and opinions toward the other, and both believe the other is the chief instigator of the error. They each wait for the other to make the first move before responding, like two chess players waiting to see what move the other will make first. Believers must remember that confession is required by the Lord not just for salvation, but also to maintain an open heaven for spiritual blessing. Often Christians want to be perceived by others as strong in faith, obedient to the Word, and living a rather faultless life. By confessing a fault, we admit we are not little angels and have not yet been glorified.

Confession is the God-given procedure for removing spiritual roadblocks out of your spirit. For example, Scripture speaks of having a "root of bitterness" that springs up and defiles a person (Heb. 12:15). In the Old Testament, the word *rebel* is used fourteen times in the King James Version and is derived from the Hebrew word *marad* (Num. 14:9) or *marah* (1 Sam. 12:14). Both words have the same root word, *mar*, which is translated as "bitter" in the Old Testament (Gen. 27:34; Exod. 15:23; Ps. 64:3).

Thus, there is a link between rebellion and bitterness. We think of rebellion in terms of being instigated by someone who leads a political uprising or by a child who refuses to listen to his or her parents. However, during my years of ministry, I have encountered bitter individuals who have remained in their bitterness because of their unwillingness to offer forgiveness or because of a situation they refuse to get over.

Perhaps we do not consider the unwillingness to forgive others as a rebellious action, and we fail to contemplate the repercussions of rebellion. Consider however, King Saul, Israel's first king. Saul was personally selected by God Himself from the tribe of Benjamin and anointed with the sacred oil. In his early rule he was dependent upon God and was "little in [his] own eyes" (1 Sam. 15:17). Saul eventually lifted himself in pride, and David was anointed to be Saul's replacement. This action infuriated Saul, and the king made numerous attempts to slay David, preventing his rise to the throne. Saul was warned not to *rebel* against the Lord, for if he did, the Lord's hand would be against him.

The favor of both God and the people was upon David, and this stoked the jealousy in Saul further. Saul disobeyed the Lord, and the "Spirit of the LORD departed from Saul, and a distressing spirit from the LORD troubled him" (1 Sam. 16:14). Saul's bitterness was rooted in his rebellion against the purposes of God, and this root defiled him, just as the writer of Hebrews warned believers it could (Heb. 12:15). As the root of bitterness produced the fruit of rebellion, the fruit of rebellion opened the door to a tormenting spirit, which battled Saul until his death. Samuel warned Saul of the danger of rebellion:

> For rebellion is as the sin of witchcraft,
> And stubbornness is as iniquity and idolatry.
> Because you have rejected the word of the LORD,
> He also has rejected you from being king.
>
> —1 SAMUEL 15:23

God will not continue to anoint and bless a person who is in rebellion against authority. Solomon also warned of the power of rebellion when he wrote:

> An evil man seeks only rebellion;
> Therefore a cruel messenger will be sent against him.
>
> —PROVERBS 17:11

The Hebrew word for "messenger" here is *mal'ak,* which has a broad range of meanings. It is used in reference to God, an angel, a prophet or priest carrying God's message, or a teacher. An example of this verse is when Pharaoh and the Egyptians rebelled against God, the "destroyer" was released upon them. The Bible says:

> He cast on them the fierceness of His anger,
> Wrath, indignation, and trouble,
> By sending angels of destruction among them.
> —PSALM 78:49

I have actually observed men and women who would consider themselves "Christians," yet they have great difficulty in getting along with others and blame their own personal issues on everyone but themselves. The excuse for swimming in a pool of bitterness is, "It was because of my mom...or my dad...or my family...or I was never given a chance by others...or I was mistreated growing up."

WHEN THE ANOINTING LIFTED FROM ME

In Scripture the jealousy of King Saul toward the youthful warrior, David, and Saul's numerous attempts to harm David grieved the Holy Spirit, causing the divine presence to depart from Saul (1 Sam. 16:14). One of the sins a believer can commit against the Holy Spirit is to "grieve" Him (Eph. 4:30) through sin, disobedience, and negative words or actions. The Greek word used for "grieve" in Ephesians 4:30 is *lupeo,* meaning, "to cause pain or grief; to distress."[2] Since the Holy Spirit indwells believers, He sees through our eyes, hears through our ears, speaks through our mouths, and is a witness to our personal actions. Thus, when biblically knowledgeable believers turn from Scripture and act in their own fleshly and carnal reasoning, the Holy Spirit can become distressed.

During my earlier ministry, and prior to my marriage, I was conducting a revival that extended into five weeks. Toward the conclusion of the meeting, and through a series of negative circumstances (caused by people's words), a division arose in the church, which resulted in two different groups verbally attacking one another, including one large group who wanted the revival closed down, and another smaller outspoken group who felt they needed a change in pastors. The final verdict of "Who is responsible for this problem?" fell on me, with the belief being that I was an instigator or at least cooperative with the group who desired a change in leadership.

Without giving further details of the matter, many unfounded and very vicious rumors began spreading throughout the denomination and among churches; all were verbal attacks upon me personally. These negative and hateful rumors were *apparently* believed by most of the ministers I knew, as proven when I attended the biannual counsel of the denomination's ministers. For five days most of the men I knew avoided me as if I had a contagious plague. Only one man, a noted pastor, came to me and said, "Perry, the Lord is with you; just keep preaching and obeying Him. He will take care of all of this."

It is one thing to hear of someone who is being ridiculed; it's an entirely different thing when the darts are flying in your own direction. After the rumors began, I tried to chase the sources down, but to no avail, and I suddenly felt the *need* to defend myself and present my side of the controversy. I discovered that chasing down a rumor was like chasing a leopard on foot—it is impossible. I became so obsessed with *protecting my name and ministry* that I would bring up the situation to people who knew nothing about it, so that if they did hear rumors, they would have the truth and not a third- and fourth-hand twisted story or someone's opinion. At the time I was twenty-one years of age and unaware that my actions and words were grieving the Holy Spirit.

When the Spirit of the Lord is grieved, He will prod and convict a person to stop his actions. The Bible calls this a case of the Holy Spirit "striving with man" (Gen. 6:3). The Spirit will plead, prod, pull, and prompt a person to turn from his or her wrong ways (by repenting) and to return to the correct path. He also gives a person "time to repent" (Rev. 2:21). In my case, I felt I was justified to make my defense as there was no one else (so I thought) who would. I knew the scriptures: "Vengeance is Mine, I will repay" (Rom. 12:19); "The battle is the LORD's" (1 Sam. 17:47); and "The LORD will fight for you" (Exod. 14:14). Yet in *my* situation God was moving far too slowly, and rumors were spreading too fast. I assumed God needed my help in correcting the situation.

While others did not notice, I began to feel the Holy Spirit and His peace and joy drifting away from me, like a fragrance becoming vague when walking away from a garden of flowers. I continued to preach, operating in the gift of communication, which the Lord had given me from a teenager. Yet I had lost the unction, the burning fire, and the anointing. My words were empty, my delivery was mere ritual, and God's peace was far removed from me. I knew the presence of the Lord had slipped from me, and I had grieved the Holy Spirit by speaking negatively about the situation, the pastor, and some of the leadership of the offending church. All of my self-defense arguments actually built an emotional pressure within me instead of forcing me to trust in the Lord. I recall actually marking the days on a calendar during December and January—twenty-one days in all—when I preached without one ounce of unction, inspiration, or anointing! It was a miserable experience, but through the battle a valuable life lesson was discovered.

God was waiting for me to repent.

I thought I was waiting on God to come to my aid and deliver me from the mouths of my enemies, when in reality God was waiting on me to line up with His word by *forgiving those* who I felt had initiated the verbal slander. My own restoration of the anointing, peace, and joy actually hinged upon my willingness to release others, which, in turn, would instantly break my own internal chains. A few weeks of misery passed, and it was January 1992 when I found myself in Daisy, Tennessee, on a Sunday night, beginning a weeklong revival in a church with about eighty older church members. It was cold and gloomy outside, and I and the people sitting in the pews were dry and dead inside. I wanted to shut the meeting down and just go home. As expected, nothing happened in the service. The following day it snowed, and the Monday night service was canceled. I remember that at about six o'clock that evening, I heard youth shouting from the bottom of the hill near the church parsonage. It was a group of friends from Lee College who were on their way to the service and were caught in the storm. They had made it there safely, but when they called back to the college, their dorm leaders gave instructions for them not to attempt to come across the mountain back to school, but to stay at the church if possible.

It was the best thing that could happen. I believe the Lord

sent that snowstorm to the hills of Tennessee that night to get my attention.

When the six teens gathered with me at the church, I went into my now sixty-days-long normal routine of revealing the attacks of the enemy and telling my details of the story. When I concluded, one of the youth said, "We need to pray about this!" Not feeling like praying, I joined in, hoping God would answer my prayer to "avenge me of my adversary" (Luke 18:3, KJV). I will always remember the moment—that moment when the fragrance of the garden returned and the sun broke through dark clouds and warmth burned again in my spirit. I was pacing back and forth in the back of the sanctuary when I heard the Holy Spirit say these words, which I recall to this day:

> Son, you need to quit feeling sorry for yourself and begin
> to think about how great and big your God is!

It was clear and vivid, and the words struck me in my stomach area, doubling me over. Within seconds I opened my mouth and declared, "You God, are the Alpha and Omega, the beginning and end, first and last…the breakthrough, the door, the chief cornerstone and Chief Shepherd, everlasting Father, Prince of peace…," and on and on the list of God's marvelous names grew. These words of praise to the Almighty felt like dipping into a pool of water on a hot day, or like a thirsty man who discovered a fresh flowing spring. I felt an inner breaking of the coldness in my spirit.

Then the unexpected occurred. Sitting at the piano was a red-headed girl named Faith. She began weeping and speaking in the prayer language of the Spirit. Suddenly a young man in the group gave the interpretation. (See 1 Corinthians 12 and 14 for more on the gifts of the Spirit.) The Holy Spirit revealed that

He had seen my plight and would fight my battle, and as a sign, in that church He would give the greatest revival I had ever seen!

Here was the enigma. This particular church had not experienced any *dynamic revival* in its history. Based on the past patterns of revivals, about 150 people would be the average attendance. I was encouraged to hear this word from the Holy Spirit, but I must confess I thought the precious one giving the interpretation had perhaps crossed from "inspiration" into "perspiration" or personal zeal.

But it was at that moment I humbled my heart to God, *repented of my negative words and bad attitude, and released forgiveness,* pleading for the anointing to return upon me and begging the Lord to perform what was spoken.

The following night the attendance was 100 people. On Wednesday it was over 200, but something unexplainable occurred on Thursday night. There were over 450 people sitting in the sanctuary. From that night the anointing returned, and I felt like Samson when the Spirit returned to him! The one-week revival was extended nightly for seven and a half weeks, with overflow attendance in each service and more than 500 people coming to Christ and 600 being baptized in the Spirit! This revival bore fruit that continues to this day, as several of the youth became ministers and today are pastors of great congregations in the nation. There were countless miracles and answers to prayer, and just as the Holy Spirit revealed, it was the greatest revival in the church's history. According to a local newspaper report, it was one of the most successful and well-attended revivals in the history of the Chattanooga, Tennessee, area.

The main lesson I learned was that God knew my situation before it occurred and was not stunned at the attacks leveled against my integrity. He desired me to walk through this crisis, as this was a trial of my faith (1 Pet. 1:7, KJV) to purge out of me anything that would or could become a snare in the future, even any form of pride. He taught me that my own spiritual freedom and level of anointing were contingent upon my willingness to hear and do His Word, and upon my willingness to always release and forgive others who brought any offense into my life.

THE GREATEST DANGER FOR MINISTERS

Based upon my personal experience and years of observation, one of the greatest dangers a minister must guard against is operating in a special gifting while living a life contrary to the Bible's standards. In today's Christian culture a natural or spiritual gift may impress observers and "bless" the people, even if the anointing is absent. For example, a gifted musician and singer with notable talent can use that talent to move people to rejoicing, tears, and other emotional responses.

However, some ministers' gifting carries them to places where their character cannot sustain them. There have been male and female ministers who could, as some say, "preach the house down," but once they left the pulpit, they would abuse the pastor's staff, argue over the offerings, and make personal demands that created havoc. One female minister built a reputation whereby she would not come to the church unless she was picked up in a particular colored limousine, and she would sit and pout in the hotel room until she got her way, often not showing up until two and a half hours after the service began. I would suggest to her that the King of kings rode a donkey into Jerusalem, and she should ride in whatever would get her to the service and be glad she's not walking to church as millions do in third world nations.

The deception of *gift ministry* versus *character ministry* is that a minister may be living in unconfessed sin or a secret bondage, and yet the gift continues to manifest, causing him (or her) to think that his actions are approved by God because the crowds are there, offerings continue, membership is growing, and everybody loves him. Samson actually proved that the Spirit's anointing will remain upon a disobedient recipient for a season despite fleshly sins and moral failures. However, eventually the Spirit of the Lord *departed* from Samson, leaving him to suffer for his folly. Samson operated in the anointing for public displays, but he never allowed the Holy Spirit to discipline him by removing the root of his attraction for Philistine women.

The anointing breaks yokes, and the same Holy Spirit who breaks the bondages over the lives of those you pray for is the Spirit who can break the chains binding *you* physically, spiritually, and emotionally. Perhaps this explains something that has puzzled many in the body of Christ. An anointed minister will preach against a certain sin, perhaps pornography or even homosexuality, yet years later be exposed in the very activity he stood against. Once exposed, ministers often say, "When I preached against the very sin I was secretly battling, I was preaching myself under conviction and would experience temporary relief from the battle." In reality, their own sermon brought a renewing to their minds, as it should. However, the speaker never entered into the higher level of personal discipline. A lack of mental or physical discipline prevented a total freedom from occurring, and when they departed God's presence, living the routine of life, the battle returned.

God's anointing is designed to "destroy yokes" (Isa. 10:27) or strongholds in the mind and spirit of a person. However, once the enemy (evil spirits) has been removed, he will make future attempts to return (Matt. 12:43–45). Perhaps this is why, when Christ expelled an evil spirit from a child, he commanded the spirit to "come out of him and enter him no more" (Mark 9:25). When Christ was tempted by Satan during His forty days in the wilderness, when Satan ended the temptation, "he departed from him [Christ] for a season" (Luke 4:13, KJV). Satan was waiting for a more opportune time to reestablish a foothold into Christ's ministry, using religious radicals and a dying thief to verbally assault Him for saying He was the Son of God. Satan's *season* struck at the crucifixion where observers demanded that if Christ was the Son of God, He would come off the cross (Matt. 27:40–42). Gifts bless people, but the anointing break yokes (Isa. 10:27). Ministers must cherish both their gifting and anointing—and guard both.

Unforgiveness and negative words will grieve the Holy Spirit, and His presence will depart. You will find yourself attempting to do spiritual work in the power of the flesh, causing weariness and discouragement. Your only relief is found in releasing your offender, praying for your enemies, and asking God to forgive you as you forgive others. I have been on both the forgiving end and the unforgiving end, and trust me, the forgiving end is the only place to live.

Chapter 15

DROPPING CROSSES

G LOBALLY, THE CROSS is a symbol of Christianity and is recognized as such even among other religions. From the ini-
tiation of the Christian faith the traditional Roman style
cross has been modified to various forms, including the Jerusalem cross, the Byzantine cross, the Saint Andrew's cross, and
numerous other forms. When most Christians see a cross, they
think of Christ's suffering. When Muslims see a cross, they are
reminded of the Crusades, and when Jews see a cross, some are
offended as they think of the Holocaust and how many of the
Nazis claimed the Christian faith. There is, however, the personal cross that each believer is to carry. Christ said:

> Then Jesus said to His disciples, "If anyone desires to come
> after Me, let him deny himself, and take up his cross, and
> follow Me."
> —MATTHEW 16:24

There are different interpretations as to what Christ meant
when He said to "take up [your] cross." In the following verse he
mentions that those who seek to save their lives will lose them,
and those who lose their lives will actually find them (v. 25).

He continues by questioning, "For what profit is it to a man if he gains the whole world, and loses his own soul?" (v. 26). The context implies that Christ is saying you must choose between loving the world or loving Him, and at times your love for Christ will conflict with the world. When you deny yourself, you will often deny your own pleasure and that of the world to choose to follow the ways of God.

However, there are other forms of a cross that people carry. For some, the cross is not just a wooden instrument used for crucifixion, but it is a metaphor for a heavy burden they must carry, one that disrupts the normal routine of life. For example, a single mother with children may find it necessary to work two jobs to meet financial obligations. Raising a handicapped or autistic child requires time and extra effort, or caring for a bedridden companion requires giving added attention that impacts the life of the caregiver. Just as believers who live in a nation that persecutes Christians continue to serve Christ out of their love for Him, a caregiver lives under the stress of a burden that becomes his or her daily cross, yet he or she performs the assignment not just out of duty but out of love and compassion.

JESUS COULDN'T CARRY HIS OWN CROSS

There are many details of the crucifixion narrative that have a parallel to the life of a believer. Christ was arrested, stood trial, was violently scourged with a Roman whip called a cat-o'-nine-tails, and was later led away to the top of Golgotha to be stretched out upon a cross and crucified. All four Gospels are united in their story of the Crucifixion. However, different writers relate the account from different angles.

Yet three of the Gospel writers point out an important incident that occurred when Christ was being led up the hill to be crucified. As Christ was led outside of the city walls of Jerusalem to the place of execution, He was so weak He was unable to bear the cross on His own shoulders. According to Scripture, a man from Africa named Simon, who had come to Jerusalem for the Passover, was pulled from the crowd and commanded to carry the cross for Christ (Matt. 27:32; Mark 15:21; Luke 23:26). John, the fourth Gospel writer, was also an eyewitness, and he describes the moment Christ took His cross and began carrying it:

> And He, bearing His cross, went out to a place called the Place of a Skull, which is called in Hebrew, Golgotha, where they crucified Him, and two others with Him, one on either side, and Jesus in the center.
>
> —JOHN 19:17–18

By comparing these four accounts, we can see that Christ began carrying His cross, but at some point He dropped the cross, and Simon stepped forward and picked it up, carrying the weight upon his own shoulders.

The pain, pressure, and weakness in Christ's body was too much for Him to pull the cross up the hill. It required someone to help Him complete His assignment of redemption. Years ago while I was meditating upon the practical application of this story, I asked myself this question, "Why did Jesus drop His cross?"

Immediately I heard this reply, "Because He knew that at times you would drop yours!" I sat silently for a few minutes and began to weep. I started thinking about various people over the years who had started out strong in the race, but because of the pain, pressure, and weakness of their flesh, they dropped their crosses. Some, like Demas in the Bible, forsook Christ because they were in love with this present world (2 Tim. 4:10). Others are like Simon Peter, who could not take the pressure of possible persecution and refused to be tagged as one of Christ's disciples (Matt. 26:69–75). Thomas saw the circumstances surrounding Christ's suffering, and based on what he saw, he was unable to believe Christ was raised from the dead. He dropped his cross of faith when doubt entered his heart.

There are times when, despite your commitment to Christ and your unwavering faith and love for God, you will have difficulty carrying your burdens and will, for a moment, feel like giving up. This is why we need not only *armor bearers*, who assist a minister in dealing with the cares of ministry, but we also need some *cross bearers* who will tell a fellow believer: "I will help you carry your burden and stand with you until the battle is over!"

Moses stood high on a mountain as Israel was warring in the valley against Amalek. Israel was winning as long as Moses held up his rod in the air. However, after several hours his hands were too weary, and he dropped the rod, causing a reversal in the war and weakening Israel. Two men, Aaron and Hur, stood under each arm to strengthen Moses to prevent him from dropping the wooden staff, which was a picture of the future cross of Christ (Exod. 17:8–13). When the rod was lifted up, victory was certain, just as when Christ is "lifted up," He will "draw all men unto me" (John 3:14; 12:32, KJV). When Christ dropped His cross, one man stooped down to lift the wooden death pole off Christ's back.

FAILURE IS NOT FINAL

Peter miserably failed, but later repented of his denials and became the voice on the Day of Pentecost to lead three thousand souls to repentance, becoming the apostle of the circumcision (Acts 2:14; Gal. 2:7). According to *Foxe's Book of Martyrs*, Thomas ended up evangelizing India, winning countless souls to Christ and seeing remarkable miracles. While praying on a mountain in India, he was thrust through with a spear.[1]

The man who bore the cross for Christ was named Simon the Cyrenian, who was the father of Alexander and Rufus (Mark 15:21). Obviously these two men, Rufus and Alexander, were known to the Gospel writer Mark, which means they were known among the early believers. When Paul wrote to the church at Rome, he said in his salutation, "Salute Rufus, chosen in the Lord" (Rom. 16:13). There are some who believe this man Rufus was the same man whose father had helped carry the cross for Christ! If this is correct, then the life of Simon, the man from Africa, was transformed when he took up the cross of Christ to the point that it impacted his own son, who also became a believer.

I DON'T WANT TO BE A CHRISTIAN

Perhaps the best way for me to sum up this book is to share with you a very interesting story. In March of 1991 I was ministering in a church in Adamsville, Alabama. Sunday morning services were always geared more for the unsaved than for believers. On Saturday night I had prepared a message that was titled, "I Don't Want to Be a Christian." The content dealt with world leaders who would have accepted the Christian faith but were hindered from doing so because of the hypocrisy they saw among Christians. That morning I preached and said, "There are sinners here who would receive Christ, but their biggest hindrances are so-called Christians. You are an elder on Sunday and at the bar cursing on Friday, and you are destroying the influence of Christ's power to deliver the lost through your public lifestyle."

I was totally unaware that on that Sunday morning was a man who was involved in numerous types of activities and whose influence controlled entire sections of the state of Alabama through his transactions. He made huge money and was a kingpin among the kingpins. Unknowingly, during my message I covered every reason he had expressed to his family for not following Christ—the chief one being, "Why should I get saved and try to do right when I go to the bar with church folks on Friday?" The lifestyle and actions of the church crowd when they were out of church did not match with the public show they performed on Sunday morning in the choir. His way of thinking was, "At least I'm a sinner, and everyone knows what I am." Thankfully the message was so on target to counter his own arguments that he submitted to the Holy Spirit and came forward, received Christ, and became a powerful soulwinner!

How many times have you heard, "The church is full of hypocrites...They are all phony...No one does what they say they do and no one lives what they are taught." The fact is that in North America many sinners have been hindered from receiving Christ by being disappointed in the double standards of so-called Christians. Despite what you hear or think, the spiritually lost individuals in this world have set a higher expectation of Christians, more so than of any other religious group.

The world is watching, and some hope we all fall flat on our faces so they can proclaim, "I told you so!" There is, however, a way to deal with the Judas goats within the church and maintain integrity and respect among the community. God never intended that the faults and failures of a few be aired as the dirty laundry on the nightly news or as a shark-fest for the yellow-dog journalists. As believers we must guard our personal lives and the lives of the sheep, and we must walk in forgiveness, peace, and unity as examples for the world to see. I have often said, "Never judge a ministry by a Judas, and never judge a church for one bad goat. Judas fell into transgression, but eleven others moved forward."

In conclusion, many years ago my grandparents on Dad's side lived in a small mountain community—Davy, West Virginia. Directly behind their home was the railroad track, and every several hours the large trains could be heard rumbling toward the town, making the ground shake like a small tremor from an earthquake. Eventually the sound filled the town, and the grinding sound of metal wheels could be heard rolling over steel tracks.

One summer I observed a dog, a rather small chap with white fur and brown spots, sitting about fifteen feet away looking up the tracks as though expecting a package from the conductor. As the train whistle blew, he stood on all fours in a crouching position, eyes firmly focused in the direction of the oncoming train. When the main engine was spotted, he began barking as if his life depended upon it. Suddenly he began chasing the train, baring his fangs, and almost snipping at the fast-moving wheels. He chased the iron beast through the town and eventually came back to his spot, tongue drooling, and lay down with his head between his front paws in an almost disappointed fashion. When the next train came through, he repeated his routine, barking and yelping as though the end of the world had come. I was amused and wondered how this little pet could even think he could slow down the train or, for that matter, stop the momentum.

At that moment I saw a metaphor. The train is the church, moving like a mighty engine carrying the gospel from city to city. The dogs are those along the path who are often outspoken and attempt to change the direction, slow down the momentum, and hinder the progress of the church. However, the church, like the train, has too much steam and fire in its belly to be stopped or hindered in its mission. Thus came this thought: "Let the dogs bark, but let the train roll on!"

After growing up in a pastor's home—where my dad pastored three different churches in three areas of Virginia, I saw the effects that mean-spirited members can have on the morale of the sheep and how they caused needless distractions for the shepherd. After observing for many years how certain members affected Dad's focus, I determined, after entering the ministry myself, not to allow man-made traditions, the opinions of uninformed people, and the negative comments of a few goats to hinder my vision or momentum. I receive negative e-mails each day, and I tell my secretaries not to bother me with someone's comments who is raving in disagreement and wants nothing but a confrontation. Some use the phone, calling our office to "vent" about a message they disagreed with and wanting to "straighten me out." Letters are written rebuking me for being wrong on my prophetic teaching.

Time is too precious to spend arguing with other Christians and trying to prove one opinion over another. I simply preach the Word and let the listeners decide. Goats will always be with us, including the occasional "Judas goat" who will eventually move into the path of betrayal. They will be known by their loud words, and they will always be giving people a "piece of their mind." The gospel is like a train that is moving full speed toward the station, and it cannot be stopped by goats, or as in the metaphor, a barking dog. Focus on the assignment, love God, love people, and let the train roll on!

Notes

Introduction

1. Wikipedia.org, s.v. "Judas goat," http://en.wikipedia.org/wiki/Judas_goat (accessed May 3, 2013); UrbanDictionary.com, s.v. "Judas goat," http://www.urbandictionary.com/define.php?term=Judas%20Goat (accessed May 3, 2013).

Chapter 1
Sleeping With a Goat in Your Bed

1. JewishRoots.net, "The Day of Atonement," http://www.jewishroots.net/holidays/day-of-atonement/yom-kippur.htm#two-goats (accessed May 3, 2013).

2. Ibid.

3. Ibid.

4. "Yoma 39," JudaismsAnswer.com, http://www.judaismsanswer.com/Yoma39.htm (accessed May 3, 2013).

5. FiasCoFarm.com, "Horns, Horn Information and How to Disbud (Dehorn) Kids," http://www.fiascofarm.com/goats/disbudding.htm (accessed May 3, 2013).

6. JewishEncyclopedia.com, s.v. "Azazel," http://www.jewishencyclopedia.com/articles/2203-azazel (accessed May 3, 2013).

7. Henry Tanner, "Pope Is Shot in Car in Vatican Square; Surgeons Term Condition 'Guarded'; Turk, an Escaped Murderer, Is Seized," *New York Times*, May 14, 1981, http://www.nytimes.com/learning/general/onthisday/big/0513.html#article (accessed May 3, 2013).

8. Alessandra Stanley, "Italians Grant Pardon to Turk Who Shot Pope," *New York Times*, June 14, 2000, http://www.nytimes.com/2000/06/14/world/italians-grant-pardon-to-turk-who-shot-pope.html (accessed May 3, 2013).

CHAPTER 2
THE BETRAYING STRATEGY OF A JUDAS GOAT

1. W. E. Vine, *Vine's Complete Expository Dictionary of Old and New Testament Words* (Nashville: Thomas Nelson, 1996), s.v. "hypocrite."

2. Based on the author's personal memory of this incident.

3. Chai Chai, "One Difference Between Goats and Sheep," *Homestead…From Scratch* (blog), May 25, 2011, http://operationhomestead.blogspot.com/search?q=difference+between+goats+and+sheep (accessed May 3, 2013).

CHAPTER 3
WHEN BELIEVERS SIN AGAINST OTHER BELIEVERS

1. EarlyChristianWritings.com, "The Didache," chapter 11, http://www.earlychristianwritings.com/text/didache-roberts.html (accessed May 6, 2013).

CHAPTER 4
WHO IS SITTING IN YOUR THIRD CHAIR?

1. Kenneth S. Wuest, *Word Studies From the Greek New Testament* (Grand Rapids, MI: William B. Eerdman's Publishing Co., 1980), s.v. "restore."

2. Lorin Shields-Michel, "Jordan Rubin's Seven Keys to Greater Health," *Healthy Living News*, April 2005, http://www.crohns.net/Miva/education/articles/Jordan_Rubin_7_Keys_to_Greater_Health.shtml (accessed May 17, 2013).

3. Vine, *Vine's Complete Expository Dictionary of Old and New Testament Words*, s.v. "fear."

CHAPTER 6
HAVING RIGHT EYES WITH THE WRONG BRAIN

1. Judy Willis, "What You Should Know About Your Brain," *Educational Leadership* 67, no. 4 (2009), ASCD, http://www.ascd

.org/ASCD/pdf/journals/ed_lead/el200912_willis.pdf (accessed May 24, 2013).

2. EyewitnesstoHistory.com, "The Burning of Rome, 64 AD," http://www.eyewitnesstohistory.com/rome.htm (accessed May 28, 2013). See also: Henry Sienkiewicz, "Burning of Rome Under Nero: Introduction," http://history-world.org/burning_of_rome_under_nero.htm (accessed May 28, 2013).

CHAPTER 7
WHEN SATAN FELL FROM HEAVEN, HE LANDED IN MY CHOIR

1. Mark Batterson, *The Circle Maker* (Grand Rapids, MI: Zondervan, 2011), 41.

CHAPTER 8
BELIEVERS WHO ARE VEXED BY A DEVIL

1. Vine, *Vine's Complete Expository Dictionary of Old and New Testament Words*, s.v. "demon," "demoniac," "devil," "devilish."

2. S. van Dorst, "The Roman Army," The Roman Army Page, http://members.tripod.com/~S_van_Dorst/legio.html (accessed May 30, 2013).

3. Vine, *Vine's Complete Expository Dictionary of Old and New Testament Words*, s.v. "vexed."

4. Ibid., s.v. "advocate."

5. Ibid., s.v. "another."

6. This information was given to the author by a source in Israel who wishes to remain anonymous.

7. ADL.org, "Tax Protest Movement," http://archive.adl.org/learn/ext_us/TPM.asp?xpicked=4&item=21 (accessed June 4, 2013).

CHAPTER 9
RESTORING FALLEN MINISTERS AND CHURCH MEMBERS

1. The details of this incident were reported and made public in several local papers at the time. To protect the privacy of the individual involved, the author and the publisher have chosen not to reveal his identity.

2. *Barnes' Notes*, electronic database, copyright © 1997, Biblesoft, s.v. "Galatians 6:1."

3. Vine, *Vine's Complete Expository Dictionary of Old and New Testament Words*, s.v. "restore."

CHAPTER 10
WOUNDED IN THE HOUSE OF MY FRIEND

1. David Maraniss, "First Lady Launches Counterattack," *Washington Post*, January 28, 1998, A01, http://www .washingtonpost.com/wp-srv/politics/special/clinton/stories/ hillary012898.htm (accessed May 31, 2013).

2. *Barnes' Notes*, s.v. "Psalm 41:9."

CHAPTER 11
THE RISE OF THE BROTHERHOOD OF BLOOD

1. This information was given to the author in Israel by an Arab source who has family working inside of Jordan and Arabia.

2. This was reported back in the 1970s by the *Atlanta Journal*.

3. The Temple Institute, "The Priestly Garments," http://www .templeinstitute.org/priestly_garments.htm (accessed June 4, 2013).

4. Rick Renner, *Sparkling Gems From the Greek* (Tulsa, OK: Harrison House, 2003), January 19.

CHAPTER 12
THE POWER OF LIFE AND DEATH IS IN YOUR MOUTH

1. The author knows Gary Townsend personally and has the information and pictures from this particular study.

2. The author knows Dr. David Van Koevering personally and has the information and pictures from this particular study.

3. Dr. David Van Koevering's website can be accessed at http://www.davidvankoevering.com/index.html.

4. The Water Information Program, "Water Facts," http://www.waterinfo.org/resources/water-facts (accessed June 3, 2013).

5. Dean Radin, Gail Hayssen, Masaru Emoto, and Takashige Kizu, "Double-Blind Test of the Effects of Distant Intention on Water Crystal Formation," *Explore* 2, no. 5 (September 2006): 408–411, viewed at http://www.explorejournal.com/article/S1550-8307(06)00327-2/fulltext (accessed June 3, 2013).

6. Zamir Cohen, *The Coming Revolution: Science Discovers the Truths of the Bible* (Jerusalem: Hidabroot, 2008).

7. Ibid.

8. Ibid.

9. Aquifers and Health Institute, "Too Much Stress Harms the Immune System," http://aquifersandhealth.org/stress-and-the-immune-system/ (accessed June 3, 2013).

CHAPTER 14
RELIEF GIVEN BY CONFESSION

1. Vine, *Vine's Expository Dictionary of Old and New Testament Words*, s.v. "confess," "confession."

2. Ibid., "grieve."

CHAPTER 15
DROPPING CROSSES

1. John Foxe, *Foxe's Book of Martyrs* (Alachua, FL: Bridge-Logos, revised edition 2001), 6.

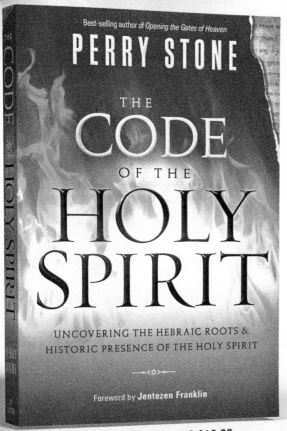

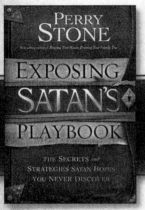